Alpha Images

Poems Selected and New

Alpha Images

Poems Selected and New

Karl Elder

Water's Edge Press LLC

Printed in the United States of America

Water's Edge Press LLC
Sheboygan, WI
watersedgepress.com

ISBN: 978-1-952526-01-5
Library of Congress Control Number: 2020945763

Cover images licensed through VectorStock

A WATER'S EDGE PRESS FIRST EDITION

for Owen and Wyatt

The Cave

Welcome. We will remain here briefly
till your eyes become accustomed to the dark.
Now, a quick word about the cave.

Observe, please, that the entrance is
no longer visible. Indeed, from this point
there is neither an exit. Take heart,

however. The tour is about to begin.
Watch your head. The ceiling is a map
that can't be read, like the innermost

reaches of nothingness sometimes dense
and sometimes dead in the water of space,
undulating and vast. Allow me

to introduce myself. I am the light
which is the voice that squats like a frog
in the form of your tongue.

I have no words for your silence.
Listen:
All around is the abyss.

Leap now or remain.

Contents

from A Man in Pieces (1994)

from The Geocryptogrammatist's Pocket Compendium of the United States (2001)

from Mead: Twenty-six Abecedariums (2005)

from The Minimalist's How-to Handbook (2005)

from A Chapbook: Some Three Dozen Miniatures from Karl Elder's Rubber Band Bound Batches of Random Locutions (2007)

from Gilgamesh at the Bellagio (2007)

from The Houdini Monologues (2010)

from Reverie's Ilk: Collected Prose Poems (2020)

New and Uncollected

Notes on Phobias
Acknowledgements

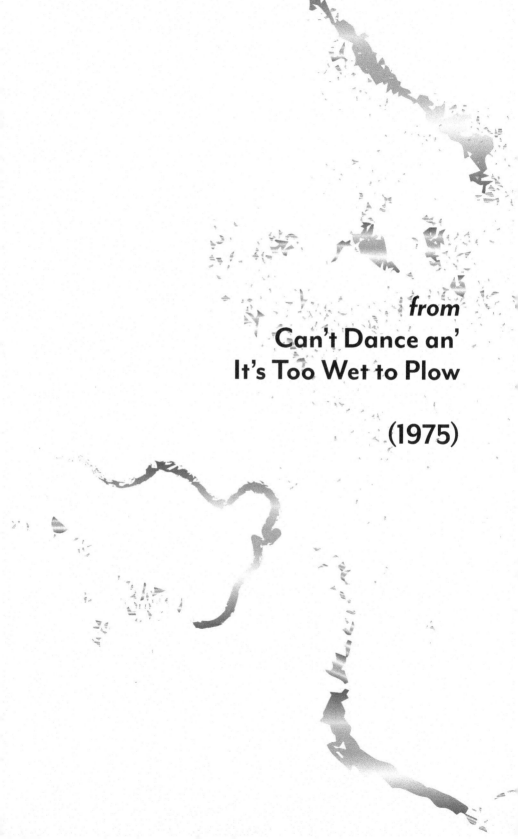

from
Can't Dance an'
It's Too Wet to Plow

(1975)

Auction

All autumn the calendar
Tells the city it's autumn
And whole households arrive
Worshipping carnival glass
Shelved like rainbows
Before their itching eyes.

From a peach basket
Tinware bursts with sun
Pooling white the palms
Of farmers' wives
That know the flat
As well as the ripe.

A Sears sack and fruit jars
Brings thirty-two-fifty
From a collector in town
And blond women bow in
Coffee steam, calculating
His fat rubber band.

International stitched
On his insulated jacket,
A man with a doughnut
Leans on the lunch wagon,
Nods how-do, and sucks
The glaze off his thumb.

Somehow Light

Somehow light takes black
Out of the imagination.
Then on the trail,
Eyes just out of the fire,
All is dark
As the tallest oak
Against the moon.
The kind that mauled
A sixteen-year-old,
Bow season, a year ago.

You knew that boy
Yet you make it no matter
While leaves
Slapping my face
Seem paws.

Even on the way home
The Utica bridge
Mouths and spits me out
At a hundred,
Trembling, thinking:
You grew out of it.

Making It Through

Here in DeKalb
The weather's
Degrees below zero.
Seems what sun
We got yesterday
Melted us in deeper last night.
The lines sag heavy
With the milk of winter,
No phones or light.

Walking to town for candles
The whiteness of cold
Numbs the eyes of sense.
Only pick-ups make it through,
Their chains
Like a scarf
Wrap a shoreline
Of crickets
Round my ears.

Truman

had boiled and whittled
a coon's prick
for a toothpick.

one March
before news reached town
the first puma in forty years
had stalked Jim French's cattle
Truman had him bagged.

he'd sit,
the juice in his cob pipe
crackling like summer weeds
and swear on a bible
he bought for the occasion
it was never him
"what left them footprints
at the ladies' winder and what
would I wont with a woman anywise?"

and later if he felt like it
like dice from his pouch
would roll a collection
of ear bones:
"these from a buck . . .
this here a muskrat . . ."
and finally what Truman
claimed, "human."

Snowplow

(for William Carlos Williams)

The blade
Scrapes sparks

How unlike
The snow

My Shoes

Like 2 mouths,
One comic,
The other sideways
In a frown.
They lay in the dark
Ready for the dawn
To swallow what keeps me up
In a play of putting them on.

Semisurreal

a crowd
does not gather.

there are only
the eggs,

dozens of eggs,
cracked or broken

bleeding
yellow on the blacktop

and the man,
the lone bald man

yards off,
squatting,

poking holes with a pen
in each end

of the one intact shell,
sucking it out raw,

studying
the giant motherload

lying on her side,
releasing

a dying hiss,
the jackknifed diesel.

The Man Who Ran

Meditation on an incident in Naha, Okinawa, 1971

that a fetus lies
curled like a slug
buried in the dank is the wonder
of what unfolds.

that he is born to light,
no root to hold him to that site,
satisfies the definition,
animal.

and that even into the night
he becomes a torch stuck in the wind,
flame pivoting furiously
in every direction—
hardly makes him a god . . .

such was the boy
burning himself to death,

fists clenched into black clubs—
on guard—
drug from the river

by those who
drove him screaming
up and down the street,

leaping,
silently off the bridge.

What We Are

the only sound a parking meter makes.
a shuffle up long stairs
to dentists' offices or
what almost makes it through
the skylight.
possibly,
even the thumbprint on a foldout.

we are nameless things:
the color of Neanderthal's eyes,
that he would be noticed
walking in the village,
his sockets small black caves.

left by ourselves
we carve the most exquisite
pumpkins, or listening to the house,
it talks, cracking its knees
as if squatting to touch
some part of itself.
one part of us laughs
it's the ghost of the
celery we eat.
the other doesn't.

or we are the eardrums,
so in the fields
we can hear the corn grow.

finally, the leaf missing,
having been blown in the mailbox
we've opened ourselves.
at dusk, the face in the moon,
indiscernible.

a few, like animals,
will escape to secret graves,
our bones used for money.

4 Shorts Concerning the President, Never Released

1

late in the oval
one night
a fly settled on my knuckles
and I did not bother
swishing it away
for the way
the front legs rubbed,
so jerkily yet so deliberate,
recalled a Charlie Chaplin movie
and that one morning
the Secretary of State went, "nya, ha ha!"

2

what I love most
when alone
is my new quartz Timex,
its mirror-like finish,
the subtle twist of my wrist
and the image bounding on the wall.

watch the man
in the third row from UPI
on Wednesday, the twentieth.

I will demonstrate
its capabilities.

3

ever had a really
bad dream?

oh I don't mean
one you imagine
you are falling
and land
but a nightmare,
a dream all of America
dreams the President
screams in his dreams.

4
yes, it is
true,

compare a photograph
of any President
before and after
and he has aged,
horribly,

but they inform me
at Walter Reed
they have developed a disease
the reverse of progeria.

in five years
I will sport pimples.

in nine
I will be gurgling
on the doorstep of the universe.

Remembering the Tennis Ball in *Blow Up*, Unable to Detect One On My Fading B&W Motorola

a novice might say
it's ballet
except for the net

and that the only muse
we hear's on the news
when the lines let

us in on what it
is the waves have quit
keeping a secret.

that is, nothing.
seems all the singing
about whether we get

an answer or not
hasn't even got
sung yet.

we are aware only
some something ghastly
hasn't been committed yet,

so locked in our room
we cut the volume.
carefully we set

the contrast just right
and switch the one light
on to get

a lousier picture.
now we are sure
even the racket

will not obstruct
the rhythm or detract
from what we have let

to our innocence.
we mumble, "what's a novice?"
and do not pretend regret.

Items

a

take the talking rain.
whatever it tries to say
forever is coiled there
at my ear bones, latent,
still.

b

the color of
electricity is orange juice.

you should have seen it,
frozen there in the toaster.

c

been thinking,
staring at the sill,
watching a tomato get ripe.

the one I already ate
tasted like a garden in my mouth.

I have visions of worms.

d

tyrant I am, all power.
a new weapon,
flipping on & off the light.
wife in bed,
I manipulate her;
at my bidding the pupils constrict,
remote control.

I walk on the blue bedspread.

e

the place is surrounded
with the ghost of Archimedes.
summers, windows open,
I've got proof:
whenever I'm hands tied,
a load to the library or laundry,
his invisibility scores again:
whap! in the ass with the door.

f

nowadays everyone's feeling the squeeze.
so when I pass through the kitchen
I rip off another paper towel,
thinking what it does for the economy.

mr. president, you must kiss me.

g

the spider I've missed killing
carries his two broken legs
close to his body
somewhere hidden in the closet.
like the bear
he is then most dangerous,
wounded.
unlike the bear he will
crawl back where I sleep
and there in my ear
lay eggs.

z

is for zodiac
or Zorro,
whichever you prefer.

I like Zorro.
the wife tells me every time
I do a dish
I leave my mark.

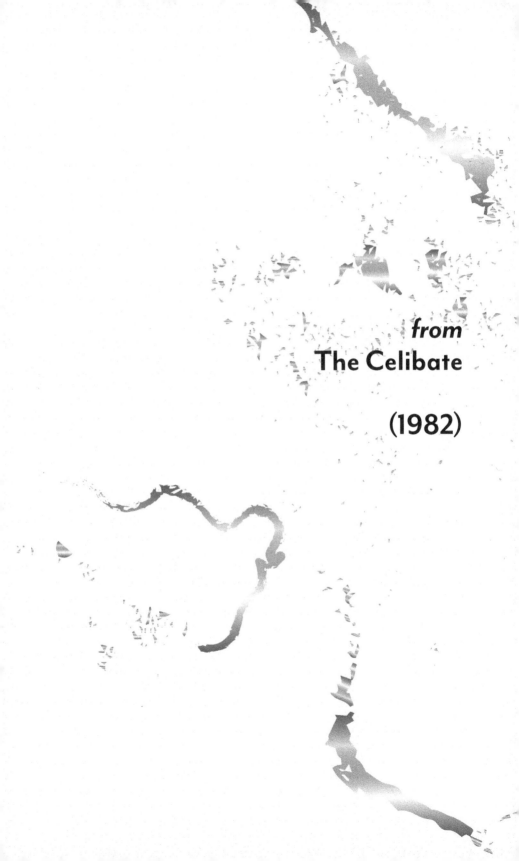

from
The Celibate

(1982)

Lightning Bug Hunting with My Niece on Her Grandfather's Farm

Town beyond the fields
like embers of a charred log,
your grandmother's mason jar,
holes for air,
a firefly,
you (Andrea) and I
are all we need.

Lying in the barnyard grass,
you whisper I must whisper too.
What shall I say?
I think only what I see:
your hair from birth,
three years long, more blond
than the Technicolor moon
and a splinter of that moon
magnified in the two
blue flames of your face
as you spy the first flash.

"Gen-tle-ly," I admonish.
"Gently," you unknowingly mock
but somehow err
as pasted on the glass
are the glowing guts of the bug
and more in your palm, face up,
dumbly wondering what has gone wrong.

"Poor bug" is the only remorse
you can muster or should.
The murder of the firefly
is the idea of the jar,
a lantern that doesn't die,
a bug I put in your head.

Fearing you're about to cry,
I whisper, "Let's catch stars instead,"
and for a moment you're willing,
perched on my shoulder, reaching
beyond your reach.

But it's a game.
The lightning bug is real,
and we're off for the corn to capture
another, a grown man and a little girl
with a kiss for me the instant we reach the fence
as if now you realize the difference.

My Ring

For Bren

Grasping
the Tao te Ching
it's suddenly there.

o

Of no use, a symbol
of what I'm used to.

o

Love.
Slipping into it,
the act itself.

o

More like a coin
than a circle;
one we've exchanged
another for.

o

And this knuckle
a monument
the finger wears
a motto for:

in gold we trust
if gold can fire
spent desire.

o

Touching you,
the hand wears a halo.

o

The ring, yellow serpent
in a gnome's den, makes
love to its mouth.

o

I imagine the flesh gone,
the bone gone,
the ring gone.

On the sink,
the worn bar of soap.

o

Lost,
I'd choose another
but love the old ring,
try to think where it's gone,
happy it's still around.

Landscape: An X-Ray

A sort of Rorschach in reverse.
Any fine line of composition
is absent—pressed flat
like a crease in a cheap pair of pants.
And speaking of pairs, there's one—
lovers in the foreground
that have to be the hips. Look,
their lips strain to kiss. But what's
this: black blotches held above—
the liver like a vile moon
and sun spots on the lung. Clearly,
nothing's in focus except
for rungs in the distance
leaning at an invisible wall
like a ladder of escape
from deepest space
or some flameless hell.
Yet here we are on Earth
the doctor's manner reminds,
measuring the pain in numbers
and degrees that reflect
perfect abnormalities.
"No doubt," he seems to nod his head and pout—
the spine is mine.

The Critter

A mistress bears you a fetus so small
she cradles it curled in her palm.

She bids that you take it home
to your wife who is childless.

"But how will she care for it?" you ask.
"Love," she insists, "conquers all."

In a couple of weeks your
wife's breasts begin to sag.

She lets herself and the house go.
She coos in the cup of her hands

and will let you hold it
only when she slips to the toilet.

One such moment a nameless dark
swaddles the house in a shroud.

Squirming like mercury under your grasp,
Baby Foetus gasps in the voice

of aborted innocence that it's cold.
You stoke the coals with your left hand

but squeeze too hard with the right.
Baby squirts out, a mess on the masonry,

a newborn pigeon on cobblestone.
Instantly you are on your knees

with tweezers, molding the globules
back in a bloodless ball

until you lift what looks like a wick
ripped from a candle—the alimentary canal.

"My God, it's gone," you wail
with something akin to grief.

"Murderer," she seethes, seated in the john,
absently unraveling a puny blue bootee.

The Celibate

A prehistory)

There is the fire you have been entrusted with,
white coals in a pouch.
There is your carelessness entering the body of water.
There is your reflection.
There is the hiss.

A history)

There are the generations which is the train
halted in the forest.
There is the beginning which is the diesel.
There is the jolt which is the sound of the theory
of dominoes running the length of the cars.
You are the uncoupling,
the dead roots of the live tree.

A future)

There is the seed within the seed which is the infinity
you are the carrier of,
the last to board the final ship
to Venus to escape a dying sun.

There is a miscalculation,
no room to seat you.

A womb)

You wander your dream which is the wilderness
finding the cave with the robe
draped over the chair.
You don it and are seated,
a black monk.

There is your dank tomb.

There are the gonads
climbing their cords to enter you.

The Laying-On of the Poem

It is the future in which
a chrome telephone has rung for days.

Your name is Jesus of Wichita,
which you gladly reveal
in want of reprisal.

Now you despise your life
you see as fog a foot deep
and dense as cobwebs
enveloping the floor of the orchard.

There is no metaphor for your pain.

You have waited too long
to explain your affection
for the balding woman
with a dolly for legs
and wooden knuckles for propulsion
on the first floor of Dillards.

You clutch her purposefully in your sleep.

Your hands are appendages for your head.

You hold a cocked analogy to her ear.

Your tongue is the trigger.

Her wits bloom into pure perception.

Dwarfed by the magnanimity of your own art,
you lay your ear snug on her sternum.

There's a stampede,
a bipedal herd of one.

The air is a dead rodent in the walls.

Five and Dime

Where nothing's a dime anymore.
Entering the store, there's the filmy
feeling the hand has
for something it wants
yet wants less to pay for—
junk a junkie wouldn't steal,
a portable TV run to a fiscal tune
of July through June,
the refrigerator hum
of a blighted aquarium in the back,
the plastic whistle of a cracked-beak canary.
From aisle to aisle, adrift in a cheap dream,
even the perfume reeks of caramel corn.
Drunk, you let the hand think for itself:
ah, dark glasses you could use,
a double purpose:
to disguise yourself,
to kill the glitter in this place—
see, finally, a familiar face,
a cardboard Leonardo's Lady
and hardly a trace of a moan
despite her yellowed lace.
You grace your jacket
with her presence,
but cave or vex,
mirrors in the corner
stare back at you like a hex
and con you into remorse,
a sort of amoral reflex.
You want to take it all back.
You take it all back.
The clerk comes to know you
for what you really are,
a customer.
She frowns at the trouble
you've handed her:
the Foster Grant's,
the picture,
Japanese handcuffs,
a squirt gun and tin star.
And for insurance

you slip a quarter in the card
soliciting for birth defects
while the cop nods his respects.
On the way out,
nonchalant,
you place a penny
on the little Kiwanis man's lip;
slowly, slowly
he's lost his marbles
and you, your grip
as the tutti-frutti bit of his brain
slips from your fingers
out the door toward the street,
chewed by another smart shopper's feet.

An Idea of Happiness

"Clear horizon; no clouds; no shadows; nothing." — *Alfred Hitchcock*

It starts off innocent as hell.

You're in a mall shopping for a razor
when in the bottom right corner
of a plate glass window
the transparent reflection
of a distant profile
steps into the picture.

The protruding abdomen and lower lip
are reminiscent maybe
of a Picasso line drawing
which causes you to turn
to find the man has disappeared.

 You turn back and find
the phantom has disappeared.

Wind chimes across the way
play a melodramatic theme.

Now you are nervous and handle your pipe
the way you might wield a revolver.

There is the little girl who saw it all,
the one you've got by the collar
while her mother mumbles,
"For goodness sake let her go."

You don't know what's come over you;
you're truly sorry, you didn't mean it,
it wasn't entirely your idea,
and you tell her so.

Next thing you know you're running;
your lungs are tattered sponges;
your heart is hitting its head against a wall.

From the beginning
you've been looking over your shoulder.

You take steps two at a time
weaving among these zombies
on an endless escalator.

Once you pass, their arms rise like a somnambulist's,
their forefingers point in your direction.

Your scent is on the air.

The hordes are gathering at the bottom stair
and coming up.

They want satisfaction.

You turn on them.

They're taken aback
and growl and scrap among themselves
for shreds of your leather jacket
you have shed in a brilliant diversionary tactic.

Your mind is a lens
which slowly ascends above it all,
through the skylight, past the low
overhanging clouds, while the scene
recedes, the city shrinks,
the continent grows small—
all contracts into a blue
and slightly oblong ball
falling into a wall-less well.

It is the inaudible plop
of the little girl's penny in water
which echoes
your idea of happiness.

The Poem Grows (or) To Help Build Strong Lines One Way

These are the wonder years,
Ages "Old Stone" through "Space,"
in which "Man," perhaps the poem
first uttered, evolves to verse,
regresses through prosody,
and breeds more verse:
"Birth, and copulation, and death."
An arrow and X-ray of my heart
for those whose art
would still propose that economy's
immediacy be subservient to breath,
but lean, nimble prose
means porky poetry
any way you pose it.
What great, hungry fate awaits? Must
The Poem never
and therefore forever stub its toe?
Or, as Poe implied, must
The Poem fast to gain weight,
methodically evading the butcher's block of time,
and thereby more effectively grow
if not more perfectly rhyme?
Even so, should we opt for either?
I think the answer yes to the latter
but confess it doesn't really matter.
The perfect poem can neither
be created nor destroyed.
Whether converted to a more
efficient form, stored
via recording or page,
or kinetic when read aloud, it falls in this age
like a dumb telephone pole
in the middle
of millions of acres of ears
of wheat,
sentencing the generator
to live out his years
happily (in Kansas
perhaps) ever after,
sullen and unheard,
and barely enough bread
though plenty of words to eat.

Poem

In love with the porch swing,
why pretend to covet
the language of coyotes?
stones?
The unawakened
dream of a geode
weathering in a creek bed.

An evening lull.

Sound of a cicada
wound like a mechanical top
and released.

Brackets of silence
around a life.

Crow's Feet

to Thomas James

No sooner than vision
began to ripen,
the ravenous black dream
straddled your eyes.

Ostrich

What a turkey!
You wade up to us
and down-periscope
to insert your weather-beaten beak
far as it'll fit
through the chain link,
me chuckling you dumb cluck,
unfolding my fist,
revealing the peanut that isn't there.
Where'd you get those peepers—
an eyebank for lemurs?
I've seen fuzz more abundant
on the heads of those
in cancer wards. Or the bald
and toothless in anti-Nazi newsreels.
Why the gnarled brown pairs
of a fused pair of overgrown carrots for toes?
What's with the bod
like a bad dream of pregnancy on stilts?
Why no remorse with a look to your mate?
Who the hell'd want that for a hat?

Always they stick you with giraffes.
Now with a camel you'd have at least sand in common,
and then there's that hose
you call a neck
practically wrapping the air
like the trap below the sink.
Where's your backbone?
Why perch here and let us call you names?
You do-do.

On Seeing Footage of the 1975 Shooting of 106 Elephants

To hell with nuclear weapons let us use elephants for bombs.
The enemy would know he'd been hit.
And when elephants become obsolete, there's always the whale.

Sasquach

for Bill Heyen

Curiosity quivers
at the chance he is near,
rears its head at a scent
as indiscernible as air,
the lure and lore of fear.

The fur-like cover of the pine
is his skin. Come dawn or dusk,
he plunges into the forest
and becomes, like all else,
the forest.

Still, men stalk him
in search of a kind of kin,
form and spirit combined like a mist
even cameras cannot cage,
a creature who has broken the bonds of extinction,

a myth that beats its chest
like thunder, moans
like the wind for a mate
and, having found a mind willing,
couples like lightning.

Born is a kind of truth:
None have reason to lie;
while man and imagination exist
there will always be a living link,
missing.

Standing in the Way of Wind

I remember Lucien mentioning
(like he assumed I already knew)
there is no music as great as wind, how
when sensing it
his hand is cutting the volume,
how with even Wagner or Beethoven
it is no contest.

Here in Kansas
I yearn for that certainty
and sing, hum—yes—even whistle
while winter branches silhouetted outside
jerk antenna-like.

What is this stuff
that it conjures the intricacy of an insect?
What am I becoming
that it no longer goes without saying
wind is the void's own voice,
that earth and water
granted the grace
something men call god gave wind,
the body might sing forever.

My Father's Dream

As heat rises,
an invisible apparition from ash,

so rose the spirit from the smoldering
body you wore like a twisted mask,

and I imagined stumbling
over you in the dark,

a great felled oak turned foxfire
life would not leave,

yet for days you lay,
as though sleep were your only success,

and wide-eyed and blind
you often woke to your own numbed voice

as if groping a glasses mirror,
a medium that you might face

this strange new innocence—the ruby,
liquid invasion of your brain,

a word your tongue would not hear of,
echo you lived in fear of

until, as a coal sparks, then flares,
your lame dream

fed it a mounting breath of air
and the word caught flame enough

for you to see to admit it,
to crawl from the cave of sleep,

to stand, to no longer dream,
to learn this new life you have earned.

My Mortality

I see where the mean (meaning average)
American adult sits ten years
in front of a TV set. I subtract
from the remainder a pack-a-day
habit, a quarter-century of sleep,
several months more for drunkenness,
and figure I'd better make this quick:

Like a cricket, the refrigerator
motor's fan belt has sung off and on
way into dawn. My thought, which now—if it
chose—might focus upon the light, is
frozen instead on how wrong (or right all
along) has been the theory of my
own mortality. I sniffle and

pout. I wring a dry Kleenex out. I learn
a drop of sorrow cannot quench grief's
thirst; it's merely the mind's means of bleeding
to cleanse the wound, reminding me of
the worst; the hurt's solely self-inflicted.
But I'm still alive. This being that is
perception fusing memory to

the moment: "It's my life," the song says; I
own it, but I can't quite con the heart
into it—a notion of dominion
as crazy as erecting a flag
in a river—splash—and for an instant
(a flash of insight sweeping me with
the current) I watch an imagined,

mute, and evaporating reflection
progressively reveal the real me,
a fine residue of brine remaining.
It hits me where I live: my life's not
mine, but in Earth's bloodstream a soluble
clot. So I feed me another line—
"Art's immortality's only means"—

and stand at the vanity, my Pentax
in hand. I nearly trip the shutter,
but it dawns on me that such portrait
is only an inverted version.
What about reality? Would the old
masters use pairs of mirrors? I give
up. I render myself in the one

mode I claim to know; I write of Washoe
the chimp, her use of Ameslan to
name herself in the glass. (And I once felt
since Man alone spoke to integrate
thought, we were in fact more angel than ape!)
There; I've got it. Perfect! Now—how to
preserve it? Ink will fade, the paper

dissolve; even stone disappears in the
end—there's no vacuum secure enough
to endure The Great Duration. Yet—
though not the parts, their sum might still be
seen—unobstructed light, a spark touched to
the future's taut and unending fuse.
I dream, having ignited that beam.

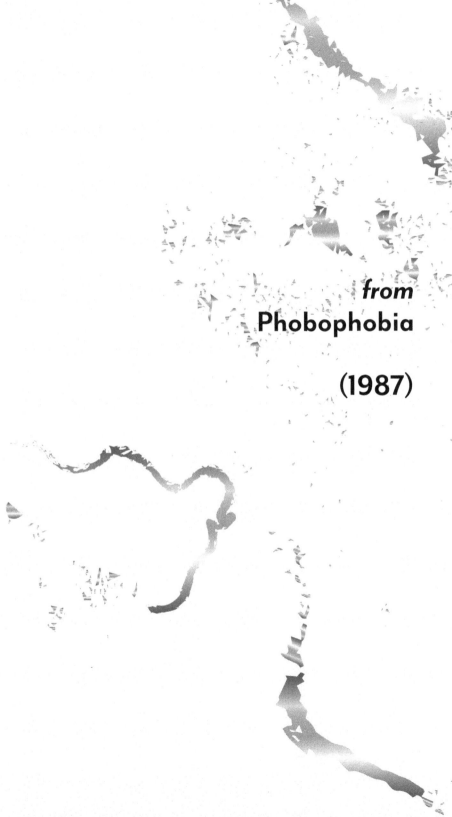

from
Phobophobia

(1987)

(Acrophobia)

"Life is just time to fill between my act."
— Karl Wallenda

But what we want to know down here
is what's death.
Something like perpetual vertigo?
The body's waters'
lust for their own level?
Or is it not that simple?
Like a life spent
trying to get your grip in a thimble.

(Agoraphobia)

Slowly purple dawns within you.

Already you wear a half dollar for a monocle.

With each step
there is the unscalable wall of a new horizon.

It hasn't occurred to you
the Flint Hills are arid,
though the buzzards have begun to circle.

Soon something like driftwood
and your numb buttocks are one.

You clutch a tire iron as if behind bars—
the penalty for conspiracy to highjack earwax.

It's hardly your fault the wheel bearing froze,
yet you would gladly confess,
if only there were another.

(Anemophobia)

Wind squeals down the flue
like hogs through a chute.

Where is your happy home,
that space you crave,
the lull between beats,
lethargic as a wall?

To run would make more wind,
but how long can your fingers
remain defense against
a noise before there were ears,
sound bound to survive all song?

It is, you recall, on wind
that buzzards are able to circle.
You try not to conjure its whistle:
interminable note of erosion
from a hollow skull below
like a pop bottle propped in a dune.

Wind will have the last word,
having been the first.

Tasteless, odorless, colorless—
the pure breath of death.

You guard your ears again,
begin, convulsively, to flap.

(Bathophobia)

You are falling in your funeral suit,
feet first, heels together,
umbrella
tucked neatly under your arm.

You pluck the petals from your lapel:

"Goodbye Grand Canyon;
see ya sunken rooms;

so long Mammoth Cave;
adieu drama in the round;

adios hot tubs;
au revoir waxed floors...."

Hello solid ground.

(Cardiophobia)

Like a bomb squad
they're back,
stethoscope pressed
to the rhythm, rhythm
until the silence
goes off in their faces and
they come alive,
knowing you're no help,
having decided to take a nap,
to have your dream
about a dead pilot light
and a dozen damp matches.

You're tired of keeping time
to that rumba across the river
now imperceptible as punctuation
in a great sweeping novel—
no relation
to the story of your life
for which the hero's demise
is predictable,
inevitable, it seems,
as the latest sequel:
even when you live
a part of you dies.

(Cherophobia)

Fa-la-la-la-la-la-la-la-la

Somehow I am both Santa
and seated on his knee.
Told to tell him my wants,
I fumble an alphabetical list the length of
and as thin as toilet paper unrolling past
the raveling row of mothers and children doubling
back beyond us, into the interminable distance.
By the time I reach "aardvark," Santa's saying,
"You've got to edit this thing, Son."
Calmly I remove my glasses:
"What do you take me for—a dummy?
I realize things like 'tact,'
'honor,' and 'nobility' are beyond your means,
but—"
He changes the subject;
he asks if I've been a good boy,
have I been eating my brussels sprouts?
I wonder aloud how'd he like
staring at a heap of the severed heads
of miniature antique mannequins.
Could Santa be an anagram
of the name of another joker
running around in red and a beard?
At that he retracts his hand, the instant
I punch him in the pillow, and I slump,
my chin on his other knee, spine limp,
stare as vacant as a bear skin rug's,
the spirit having abandoned the body.

(Claustrophobia)

It is with great patience
the mind has tolerated
the blue suits, the few
pair of shoes, even the prom dress
you now squeeze out of
with extreme reluctance.

The batteries begin to dim.

Once more you try the door.

The floor-length mirror,
an old friend,
is fading fast.

You grasp the flashlight
as if to eat the beam.

When you blow out your cheeks
and belly just right
you can almost see it:
the skeleton key
swallowed in your childhood,
slowly digesting.

With nerves of iron
you brace yourself against a premonition:

you will live forever.

(Coprophobia)

You hear the choke, the final slosh, think
as you were hypnotized to think
it's the flush you dread about a toilet,
the cold chrome of the trip
like a key to an instrument
whose only music
is at once hoarse and metallic
as the sound of a jet
honed from lead to a fine shiny tip—
opposite the Doppler effect.

Later, leaning over your morning coffee,
you're reluctant to call your cup a puppy,
but there's a puddle under it.
And you're not about to mop it.

Here you remember your dream
in which your analyst invents a scheme
to measure your fear.

He stands on a tapped keg of beer
outside a circle
the center of which is a bucket.

He blows his whistle:
"All right, men," he yells, "fill it!"

The last one done runs him the pail,
hangs it from a nail
just above a trough,
gingerly, so as not to spill it.

Old stoic that he is, the doctor
posts no demonstrator,
but adjusts his goggles, the ear
and nose plugs, dunks—up to the Adam's apple—
his head in the bucket.

Made to weigh the run-off,
you know it's the standard by which
forever you'll be judged.

(Emetophobia)

Aren't you blessed
gravity doesn't pull from the west
that dust settles on surfaces
where it's easy to dust
and not on walls.
What a bitch to yell duck
every time you dropped your fork.

Think of spilled milk
streaming like a tattered flag of truce
across the kitchens of the Earth.
Think of caviar impossible to keep down,
of despair which owns a gravity of its own.
Say hello to portholes for toilet bowls,
goodbye to looking your patients in the eye.

(Graphophobia)

A man, who is not a mime,
thumbs pages of air.
He is grateful for the little
out-of-the-way store
which carries such exquisite work
and thankful to the publishers,
whoever they may be,
given how faint the imprint.
Like him they see it
a fresh breath of air
for which their offer,
unreal that it is,
lies unsigned in a vacant drawer
near a wastebasket
overflowing with more air,
which the man who is not a mime
has yet to fill,
typing, so to speak,
without benefit of paper
the most novel of novels,
wadding it all, sheet
after immaculate sheet,
in such a furiously small ball.

(Hierophobia)

Awash in these
waves of faces
like a bottle without a message
but its bobbing,

about to spill the
fermented memory
of the sanctuary where you suffered
total immersion,

up off your knees,
foaming at the mouth
as if the pastor set an Alka-Seltzer
on a sweating tongue,

you see they see the
sheen of your psyche,
this scene you can repress no more
than a fishbowl

can its wall, a
pinball its chrome,
a Gypsy's crystal its fate to reveal:
a soft cross above

a warped pulpit and
rubber altar before
banners made of whole bolts of felt;
elastic velvet over

platters for plates
under wax melting fast,
its light like that of the stained glass
like invisible wet paint

like the antithesis
of the dry portrait
of the same silent barker who doubles
at the dunk tank.

(Ombrophobia)

All afternoon a rumbling
burping blue.

You hated the bass drum in high school,
you hate it now,

crouched in crackling news,
sniffing the ground
surrounded by toppled chairs
and pairs of binoculars
on the grandmother's lawn
where the granddaughter lay
skewered by lightning.

It is the day following,
July the 5th.
You drive as if
on a great dumb tongue,
wheat stacked
in every direction.

Then green,
green,
all is an ill yellow green.

In the rearview mirror
on the horizon—a funnel
like a uvula in a comic book frame
for which you need no bubble
to read the scream.

(Ornithophobia)

You're hardly baby Audubon
as you crane with the inevitable question:

"But where'd the stork come from, Mommy?
Wait, don't tell me—where eagles abscond
with bad little boys."

Things out back are ominous too.
This small black flock
hovers, darts like
an omnidirectional craft,
then folds like a wing
on the neighbors' antenna.

Could it have affected reception
of the scene of Tippi Hedren
smoking on a park bench,
her back to monkey bars
quietly becoming a roost
for what seemed a whole species?

Time has come and gone
when bird meant pigeon,
those coos as soothing
as a scuba diver's breathing.

There is instead frantic wheezing,
the scar of that film,
that scare you wear
like a condor on your shoulder.

(Polyphobia)

This is the lake in which you jump
to get in out of the rain.

Here is the line in which you stand
as a form of recreation.

These are noon whistles
that sound "lunch" to even you—
the howl of a pack of predators.

Once sweet, your love is like plaque;
you brush her before bed.

You question the compatibility
of hell and high water.

Lightning lights like a graph in the sky.

Window panes flash your distress.

You carry in your wallet
the photograph of a splash,
a synthetic wing,
the germ of your plan for a new species.

You've been waiting for something big.
Like a new kind of bomb.

You hold your breath for lent.

(Rhabdophobia)

Poe scholar by day,
bricklayer by night,
leaning,
hands over your ears,
forehead against the wardrobe,
you mumble as if asleep,
"Two-hundred twelve—"
"What?" yells the cop.
The jackhammer stops
and suddenly,
here in your room,
it is hailing
and then it is not.
You, the cop, the hard-hat
and moth balls a foot deep.
You swallow hard before you speak:
"bones in the body."

(Sciophobia)

Ha, shade! Euphemism for
shadow, part of the dark

dank tunnel you've traveled
since your boyhood room where

the mirror might as well've
faced the wall,

so awful it was
to look upon glass

that seemed, like Dracula's,
unable to reflect. There

a shadow lurked in the shadows
cast by the streetlight

a B·B shot out
every other night

that time you felt mean,
man, real mean—

the very same shadow
you lie on now

like the ghost of somebody else
in this two-bit rented room

in the cool of an awning
where you are bored,

boy, bored beyond yawning,
having been tailed,

targeted from the beginning
victim of nothing,

your self the weapon
of its would-be assassin.

from
A Man in Pieces

(1994)

Immersing a Sand-Coated Hand in Water

for Dave Lauer

Done with all that fuss at the office,
here with the kids, back of the house,
kneeling before a bucket by a big old tire,
glove of grit to the wrist.
How could anyone earn this moment—
like swirls of flesh unfurling
soon as my hand is under,
how it would have to look,
feel,
entering the afterlife:
the spirit smoldering,
quenched.

The Day of the Night

The picture I hold in my head
is of my father as a young man
in uniform in Australia.
He is healing slowly,
though in a few days he'll be released.
You can see in his face
he's tired of all this,
wants it how it was
on the islands with Bill,
his buddy even before they went in.

Divers before the war —
hard helmets — then sailors
in the South Pacific
in the middle of a night
with orders for a tiny island
where, off shore, short of the runway,
yesterday's plane went down.
There were nurses aboard — seventeen,
one engaged to the Captain.

The day later Dad needed sleep.
He said he told them
he couldn't go on.
He said Bill said nothing.
He said they both kept puking.
At first in their helmets.
Then dry heaves.
But the sea was calm.
Word came down.
They would go
until the last bloated body was brought up.

Returning to the submerged plane
was like sleepwalking.
And what is a dream
but being able to breathe under water,
a nightmare but what they saw,
the cock-eyed fright in the face
of those who died before the drowned,
the limbs by now
permanently out of place.

They pulled them by their hair,
tied them by their ankles, their wrists —
whatever worked to work them loose.
The equipment was makeshift.
It did damage to the flesh.
The lines intertwined.
They were lucky to get them out in time.

Yet they weren't done,
my father and his friend —
escorted to separate rooms.
Hours later they still weren't done.
The Captain had one question:
"Which one of you has got
the Goddamned diamond?"

I don't know that Dad saw his friend again.
It was how my father made it to Australia,
the one time he's talked about it
and the plane
and the hypnotist-psychiatrist,
twenty-five years later,
the summer I turned twenty-one,
the morning after we'd mowed the lawn,
sitting in the kitchen,
the day of the night
a stroke split his tongue.

Lilacs

1.

Heading downstate on the blacktops in May
great bouquets of them
set along the farm lawns,
umbloomed up home,
here blossoming,
then the fluent scent, the white,
the pale and the deep full clumps of purple
until finally you need only breathe
to sense you ride the crest
of an imagined wave.
You think of the backwash,
how the color each variety's
been selected to reflect
does its slow ripple north
like the season.

2.

Lilacs. The very word is a spring song.
And because they arrive untended,
like spring itself,
we relish the gift,
wanting to own them,
knowing such is imposible
even with the cultivated—
the tulip, the iris—
so unthinking are we to snip the sprig,
strip the bark,
stand them in water,
making them as common
indoors as out,
where they're quick to wilt.

3.

Yet it's their impermanence that saves us
for want of another spring of them,
makes such plentiful perfume so precious.

Think of a painter,
palette in one hand, knife in the other,
so drunk with their fragrance
he is seen wandering in circles, blind.

Lilacs. You sometimes think
they are the art of the earth.

Diary of the Stone

#

Gravel snaps in the wake
of an infinitely slow wheel
wobbling on a bike
I hike beside,
sound of brushfire
too green. Dusk barely contains
the illumination of the lane, dust
soon phosphorescent
as if a fault in the night
or floor of a tunnel,
the huge corrugated tile
I pulled my son from
where his mom found a stone
smooth as an eraser
I keep warm between my forefinger
and thumb.
I think of every wad of clay
or gum this size I've
pinched this way, wanting play
in the form of the stone. Nothing.
Only the sense of touching another
when touching something of your own
gone numb.

#

Later I sit smoking in the dark.
An imperceptible rain has begun.
The mercury yard light hung on the barn
seems ordinary as a star.
Today Gerard told me he got to touch
a moon rock. And though he didn't say,
I know how he felt.
Like he just stopped crying.
He said he was moved by it,
there in the museum. A confession by one
some might call immune to affection.
I hold the stone,
impenetrable as my friend,
flawless as the texture of any woman.

\#

Months now and the stone
surfaces in the phone drawer.
How right the urge to invent a fiction—
return it to the farm,
bury it like the coin
I would as a kid,
a cinch I'd be back.
But first I must own the stone,
have it sewn to the lining, so to speak.

\#

Love the constancy of the stone.
Each moment I watch
a clone of the moment before:
light from the other room,
that nothingness the stone wears,
sheen of skin so taut
it could heal quick as a cut.
I pick it up, rub
an infinitesimal dust,
reliving the touch
of my newborn sons.

\#

This stone a bone cell
were the planet a skull &
or life form
entombed by its own skeleton,
dungeon of stone
entombed by its own skeleton
or life form
were the planet a skull &
this stone a bone cell.

#

Stone like a koan
where I keep you now
as if to guard the negative
of a discarded snapshot
of a random point in the universe
common as any other,
as all the space possible to imagine,
like that between galaxies,
without substance, without dimension without
a mind to meld mind and stone.

Cutting Pigs

Never really cut, only caught
and held them for the farmer's kid,
whose blade was curved and quick.

The rest is haze
alight with an awful squeal,
but for the dog outside the fence,

who leapt for his breakfast,
caught it on the fly,
ate till he retched,

then snapped at a dozen more.
I was a townie and this was a rite.
Who for, who could be sure,

though sometimes since
I sense this twinge
(far from guilt for the geldings):

a flurry in the scrotum
so that I picture a farm,
an aerial view of a surge of sperm.

As to remorse or even regret—
like the farmer said,
"A barrow is born to be et."

Larry's Fina

"The one thing good about Kansas
is Coors," my brother-in-law says
while Gary, his neighbor, shifts gears
and I drink to that. "Sweetens
the breath, loosens the bowels,
and makes childbirth a pleasure."

This afternoon's object: to get
a guy named Larry snookered
and us back with firewood in the truck bed
and money in our pockets to prove it.
"Candy is dandy, but liquor is quicker."

A sixpack later, we swing over ruts
in Larry's driveway and park by the pumps.

Larry's son is Little Larry, shooing
the summer's surviving fly
landing on the lip of his Pepsi.

Larry is fat, but after a few beers
light on his feet, bitching about
the high cost of wiping one's butt.

But there's something to be said
for the firewood he sells he says.
Larry wants fifty bucks a cord
for oak, provided you haul it.

Gary thinks that's steep, but maybe
Rick, Karl's brother-in-law, Vice
President in Charge of Bullshit
for Stanley Tools, can work something
out. Larry doesn't laugh.

Toying with a sample of his trade,
Rick asks Larry if he's a tool nut.
Larry says no, but he'll take forty-seven
fifty cash money if we fill the pick-up with gas.
We do, but before it's over
snitch an extra corner off a rick of hickory
and talk him down to forty-two.

A true cord is four by four by eight
Little Larry says and uses his new tape rule
to prove it, while we, with something like
water in the tank, buck and chug onto
the highway, fishing under the seat for
more suds to commemorate "A good job done."

Constanza

This strange young woman with her black dress
and olive complexion accepts the offer
to walk her home. It is clear her classmate
is interested for the right reasons, clear
as the night itself is clear, since hers
is not the face of a white boy's dream,
though endowed with a divine symmetry.
The looks the student yields are proof
he is drawn by something within her that,
were she to show it, he could know love.
The second time around her block
the young man is unaware they have
arrived at her neighborhood. Neither
does he realize they have attracted
an escort of young males, so absorbed
is he in the woman's sweet voice
flecked with nuance from her native tongue.
All the while it is he of whom she speaks,
both a sign and cipher of her pure
intentions, which he senses she is always
about to reveal, as these walks go on
all summer. Suddenly one evening
she grasps the man's forearm, standing there,
gazing skyward. There is in the faces
of those who surround great anticipation.
Constanza is her name, and it appears
she would be hard pressed to hear it
were he to speak it, even now as
she turns toward him to say goodbye,
there before the stoop of her building
where her mother and grandmother sit,
awaiting her return, though on this night
the steps are bare, as are Constanza's wide,
angular shoulders and buoyant breasts,
for she has deftly, without encouraging
passion in him, disrobed herself entirely

to the waist. The young men, as well as others
who have spontaneously gathered, kneel
all around, crossing themselves over and over
again. For the briefest moment, then
during one prolonged gasp from the crowd,
her back turned as she ascends the stairs,
the shoulder blades twitch, then contort,
begin to stretch the lavish skin so that
the boy knows he must go to her
yet first scale wonder akin to horror.
There is pain in her face as she turns
at the top of the steps to receive him,
her arms by her sides, her hands held
before her abdomen, palms up, so that
the young man need not immediately acknowledge
she now has wings, wings like in the picture
of the sculpture with wings he has seen
in the class, marble wings all the more prominent
with the head cut off.
And the boy knows her beautiful skin too
is becoming marble, though still animate,
still human enough, still woman enough
so that before, as an old man, the boy dies,
he tells of their marriage bed, the two
magnificently healed scars like melted wax
on her back, and the pair of white butterflies
having mated to produce black offspring
to rest upon and completely conceal
the likeness of Constanza above her grave,
white butterflies that sprung one at a time
from her labia, he insists, that first
night, before they made love.

The Inevitable

"If you wanna get to heaven, gotta d-i-e.
You gotta put on your coat and t-i-e."
— Waylon Jennings

I.

I am greeted by a chauffeur
whose hand holds the latch

to the rear door
of an orange, windowless hearse.

It's so black and bottomless in there
I figure somewhere

there's got to be a gun:
I enter. Now I am weightless

and worry any matches in my pocket
will prove useless.

For the life of me
I can produce only one.

II.

In a moment I have by bearings—
I'm at the foot of a satin canyon.

Faint clouds the shape
and consistency of shrouds

drift the unnavigable dark, their motion
as ineluctable as a shark's.

I suck sharp pain
from my thumb and finger

while the wick of my spine
flames with black thoughts.

III.

I learn endurance,
bobbing in the deprivation of my body.

The driver becomes my confidant.
I confess my wish to be like

everybody else, that I sincerely
cherish anonymity, that without it

I might perish. "Believe in me,"
I read in a kind of Braille

from the dimensionless medium of his lips,
"and you shall dwell forever

in absence." I contemplate:
can nothing occupy space?

I billow like a sail.
I cast the anchor of my will.

Four for Mario

I.

Suddenly a poem seems dumb.
Maybe like you I'd rather perform:
I rehearsed a week to tell my son
of your death. I learned by heart
how not to speak, to trust my tongue.
He waited until I was done.
He stared at me across the room
as I cradled my younger one.
He loves you, he said.
Even dead.

II.

The pictures didn't turn out,
though I can picture each frame:
Seth, your understudy, your "main
man" in your lap.
What a team of dreamers!
If only we had a script, you said,
there'd be money enough to keep him in Underoos
and us in booze
till hell froze over.

III.

It's been a bitter winter.
We play the planet Hoth.
Seth is Luke, I'm Vader.
Once through my mask
I heard hint of your voice,
and, once, stung by a gust,
I spun, sensing your form, your shadow
near snow packed high by the plows,
iced all over, glistening
like a huge granite boulder.

IV.

A man enters the shadow of rock
and the shadows are one.
Black is our shadow on the moon,
the shadow of Earth,
which is the shadow of rock.
Black, which is the color
of every man's shadow.
Black am I there who here am white.
Black like my brother,
you, who called me Brother.

The Searcher

*"This is embarrassing... but I can't find the way back
to my new home. I've searched and searched."*

Norwegian JERMUND SKOGSTAD, who took a break from moving into a new
Oslo apartment, went out for a bite to eat and forgot to take his new address with
him. He has been looking for his apartment for more than a month. (*Newsweek:*
October 15, 1990)

I am not blind;
I know my life
will never be the same.
A thousand times
in a thousand directions
I've counted the steps.
When I open my eyes—
should I be surprised?—
the latch is gone.
Or wrong.

Maybe what I've
needed all along
is a phone
minus the hotel room.
I think of walks
in search of sound:
I dial the apartment.
I let it ring.

I'm running low on funds.
Soon I'll own
two of everything
and one of some
that make me a stranger
to the place I belong:
a map, a compass,
a reply should I
receive a welcome:
"A pleasure to meet you, too.
I'm the new night watchman.
Why I'm never around
is I moonlight by day,
guardian of my own thick sleep."

I've known women
like my new home.
Lately I dream about
one that got lost
on our date.
When I awake
the fold in the pillow
I still probe is dry, and I,
I am spent. It's the sense of
when a mother
won't have you back.

I remember
that as a child
I played with my father's keys
at his feet.
Now I have a set of my own.
This is the one to my apartment.
Please.
Take my hand.
Help me up off
my literal
metaphorical knees.

The Bystander

NEW YORK (AP) – A woman who was bouncing on the bed of a New York City hotel plunged to her death from the 20th floor when she bounced out the window, her husband told police.

Police said Sylvia Maninirios, of Montevideo, Uruguay, was found dead early today on the sidewalk outside the Taft Hotel in midtown Manhattan. Her husband, Bruno, 29, explained she had been bouncing on the hotel room bed and accidentally bounced right through the window, police said.

Maninirios was held for questioning, police said.

Don't bug me.
I got grief enough—
the only child of a mother
who died in childbirth;
a son of the son of a bitch
who left her.

I'm five when a Sister sees me
biting the head off a dead fly.
I think it's a raisin—see?

At ten they caught me again. It
was already dead; I swear
it was a marshmallow peep.
Who'da guessed a canary?

We're playing vampire, my friend and me,
but neither's got the guts
to even fake
it with the stake.

Soon it's Robin Hood.
We fire an arrow in the air, straight up,
then drop on our backs to see who's chicken.
That was his mistake.

I tell you God's against me,
the Devil too. Believe me, I tried
time and again to x this jinx.
But the weapon was wrestled from my hand.
It went bang.

One by one, some nuns turn up missing,
and the cops wanna know
where I get all the black
rags. Finder's keepers.
Tomăto, tomäto.
Their "rags" are my flags.

So I'm here on business.
So my wife believes in insurance.
So what?

Firebuck

One antler purple and orange flames,
the other yellow, sheathed in soft blue at the base.
This I confirm with my son, straddling my knee,
authority in these matters,
since I'm a bit blind to color.
At three he thinks nothing of it,
my only failing. I love the red in his hair
like the late afternoon sun in his mother's,
I think, turning back to the fire.
And as memory makes magicians of us all,
I conjure again this animal,
its rack refueled by another log I've lain.
Now the flames flap
like wet shirttails in the wind
and I who ride
am for a moment myself,
the child content with the man he became.

from
The Geocryptogrammatist's Pocket Compendium of the United States

(2001)

AK

Alas shall be first.
Phantom anagram? Pun? Yes,
paradise on ice.

AR

State of being here—
no modal, no transitive,
no intransitive.

AZ

Arid alphabet
and desert's dictionary
of all nameless space.

CO

The first o a hole
in knowledge how to pronounce
en español, o.

CT

The feature's trailer:
Your scene with the net cut cut
and therefore the plot.

FL

Shall we compare thee
to a Stevens trope? Thou art
more fiction less hope.

ID

Mind's old ruins or
map that says you are here no
matter where you are.

KS

This is existence?
This is a box of Wheat Chex.
Kiss your is goodbye.

KY

No trifle, the key's
tuck in and squeeze with no bead
on a long rifle.

LA

Dear Monsieur LaSalle,
Tell Louis we had to sell.
In hell, Bonaparte.

MA

Mammoth, Mayflower—
alternatives among sets.
You get to choose. Pick.

MD

Sorry, Doc, to break
the news. It's your appendix.
We gots DC blues.

MI

Myocardial
infarction: 1,001
Edsel sales then none.

MO

Marauders'
modus operandi: Motive means
opportunity.

MS

Married or old maid?
In whose mansion you sip tea?
In the one you pee?

NH

Something there is loves
its wall to Washington and
ladder with one rung.

NJ

Philadelphia's
waterboy, New York's farm team.
Which side are you on?

NV

No silver sliver,
this potshard in the crook of
California's arm.

OK

How the mailman knows
you're giving him the nod, you
mean this address, yes.

PA

Whose words these are pen
thinks it knows. First came woods. Then
etymology.

SD

"Corn Palace?" "Wall Drugs?"
"Drive," he sd, "for Christ's sake, look
out where yr going."

TX

Christ down off his cross,
the big piece of the puzzle.
Brand and snapped handle.

UT

University
of Technicolor. Bible's
lot. Cowboy's backdrop.

WA

As in gorge, of course.
Think rain rushing down Rainier.
No misnomer here.

WV

The cartographer's
idea of toad, one leg
tucked under a board.

WY

Because it is there.
Because there is also here.
Is everything square?

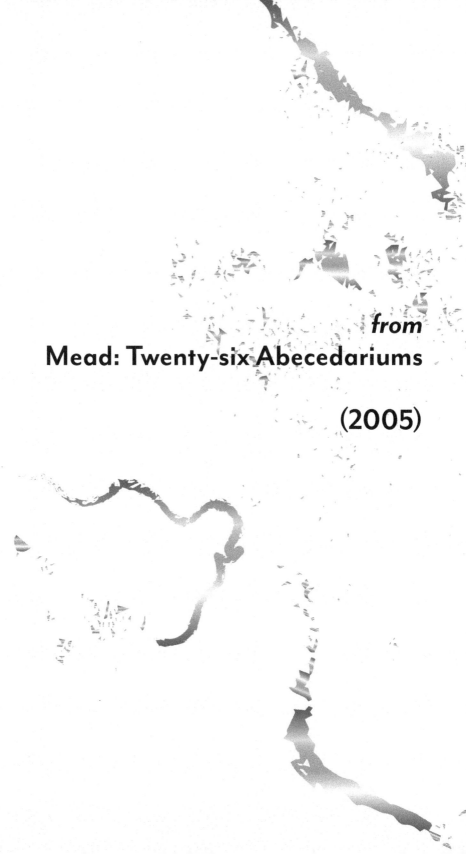

from
Mead: Twenty-six Abecedariums

(2005)

Original Sin

"A ain't just for applesauce, the alpha
bet Adam, who bemoaned the fact they were
classmates, of the same school, no less, Adam
dumb as he was, as Alf was smart as. "In
each of my hands," Alf then posed, "I hold peach
fuzz but no peach. Now what," he said, "have I
got?" Adam's eyes jerked side to side as if
his head were caught in a vice, the riddle
inside, as if Eve might have the answer,
just over his shoulder, mum. "My word, what
kind of conundrum have these two cooked up?"
lisped Adam as though a condom sheathed his
mother tongue or a code invaded his
nose. "Come home hungry and what do I get—
original thin and a thickening
plot, as though Elmer Fudd's become my lot."
Querulousness being father of prayer,
right away the Good Lord God Almighty
spoke: "Good grief, man, as though that knot in your
throat were not enough, you're clueless too. Your
ewe is lost, your luck is fucked, dah dah dah/
dit dit dit dah/ dit/ dit dah dit." Adam
wished he'd been born all alone. Now, rated
X, with no recompense, he in his myth
yammers on, stewed with the sour juice of
Zeus—how he might have made him president.

Everything I Needed to Know

Ashes, Ashes, we fall on our asses
because the teacher has us. Rodeo
clowns make about as much sense, but then they
don't graduate from kindergarten that
early either. Neither could they have had
for their teacher Mrs. Cunningham, whose
grave countenance no kid had the word for:
Her is no bull sitter. Her is squeezing
in chair, knees together. Her is a locked
jaw with lips like a bad ventriloquist's.
Kind of like a lady Clutch Cargo. Or
like the bride of a Nordic Frankenstein,
motherless but blonde, beautiful, and big.
Nobody here knows she has another
occupation but me. I'm her little
Picasso, her baby ham, and cunning.
"Quit staring, Karl Curtis," she says, looking
right at me. She knows I know for a split
second she disappeared and does not want
to reveal her secret identity
underneath. I know she knows I draw some
very naked ideas. Later, when
we go around and tell in tones like the
xylophone's, girls always first, what it is
you want to be when you grow up, I say
Zorro because a poet needs a mask.

Anna Banana

A. B. C. D. E. F. G. H. I. J.
Bird. What's a J-Bird, anyway? How'd it
come to be naked? Maybe it's a she.
Does she live in a tree? A. B. C. D.
E is for Eve, whose apple isn't just
for her, the teacher, especially when
getting her pupil's goat's more savory.
Here's a little ditty: 1. 2. 3. 4.
in a boy child's best prepubescent voice.
Jump rope's like that. They've got you hopping, then
K-I-S-S-I-N-G in a tree.
Lust? Ask around. On any playground *like*
means love. Love is yuck. Strictly for grownups.
No respectable kid carves or draws hearts
on oaks or walks if the object's not to
pimp your buddy. As for girls? Few are the
queens keeping to an airy castle while
royalty's right ventricle's still AWOL.
Surely goodness and mercy shall follow
them, female and male, Jill and Jack, up, up,
up the hill and back, back, back until all
virtuosity they once lacked appears
without warning to dance, dance away doom.
X, God knows, is but one sex chromosome.
Y is why it takes two to fandango.
Zoom in. Zoom out. Big and small, they're human.

The Resignation

Ace-deuce-tray-lady-kink—another hand
busted before it began. If the whore
could have only come up a four, your king
down, dirty as it may be, might have been
enough to best the better, to call his
flush or shush a bluff in this two fisted
game named stud—misnomer if ever you
heard one. Pud poker would be more like it—
aye, Mate, even Watergate, a ship you'd
jump but didn't dare, your stroke weak as your
kick. The captain—alias luck—has you
lashed to her mast. You're her chump, her Richard
Millhouse Nixon, not one known to know a
noose from a knot. Still, once upon a time
once a month while a sailor in the South
Pacific, seemed you sent home every pot—
Quaker or not. It's how you financed the
race, your California congressional
seat. It's how you came to be beat then won
the presidency to lose it again.
Us? We all were winners and losers too—
voters with a voice, finally, as you
waved the sign for peace, arms a V then an
X, that nix, that quick fix, ducking from sight.
You understood the Law of Averages.
Zapruder, after all, might have filmed you.

Tall, Dark, and Handsome

A look on three women's faces enough—
by Christ enough—to make ten men jealous;
caught in a wave of quiet wails, the word
dead bobbed to the top, sank, and suddenly
everything there in the checkout line stopped.
For a second I thought the president
got it. Who would have guessed the king instead?
How were subjects in Springfield, MO to know
in the first place he was ill? Heavy? Yes.
Just a tad bit overweight. Yet still those
keen tabloid-cover collars, that killer
look I, at nine, commenced to cultivate,
my mother's mirror seemingly etched by
none other than his image, his svelte voice
on in the background and my face in the
proscenium in spite of the flaking
quicksilver, comb in one hand and white and
red crimped tube of Brylcreem in the other.
Sculpture. Pure sculpture. Adonis with duck
tail. And that part I played in the play—no
understudy for a half-tragedy
vied more for the role, his tale with a tail,
with a tailor whom, should the body be
exhumed, we'd call The Cat That Gave the King
(Yancey? Lansky) His Cool: white suit, white shirt,
zaffer tie. To die yet glow in the dark.

The Chills

Awe, we know, is opposite of *ennui*,
beauty being the form, the good worm to
churn the soil of even the darkest souls.
"Dig, thus, your own grave to dance upon it,"
every poet I've dug from Poe on down
forewarns. Yet it's not lore for which I bore
goosebumps today, the first time in months, nor
horror before a mirror, but love of
inspiration, insight flying blind like
jagged lightning, mind to mind, across a
kindred sky. Alone on my way home, a
lull in an otherwise dull day at work,
my finger hits the PWR button and,
now, like the air bag went off, something like
ozone fills the van, liquid emotion,
perfection in the raw that saw—you can
quote me—hair stand in my ear to then lean,
reaching for the origin of the storm,
speakers speaking in tongues, licks electric,
tons of nuance and that shrill demand you
understand: "I am what I am, Edward
Van Halen." I thank God for the goddamned
wonder of it, that energy, the gift,
x for all your problems solved if only
your answer were not a mystery, that
zone more like home than the earth where you live.

Transportation

A car should take you where you want to go,
boast a bit of personality, but
claim no soul. So why so hollow having
done away with this one, a van, sold—not
expunged like the rest, towed I mean, more beasts
for the bone yard—when a hundred thirteen
grand ought to be enough for anyone.
Here we're talking miles, of course, not moola:
in ten-plus years four trips around the world.
Just think of the tenths. Figure the inches!
Kept I it another minute, why I'm
likely to have done run out of road or,
more likely, luck, luck being a function
no less of grace than of space to live it.
O for another junket in my junk—
PT Cruiser be damned—though I had no
qualms the moment I signed, sacrificed all
rightful claims in exchange for money down.
So I scrawled a second time, transferred the
title to a John Someone whom, you'd think,
you might recall his entire name except,
very sudden, dumb as a manikin
with seizures of sentimentality,
Xmas come and gone, you, I, you, you chump
you, are transported here, an untethered
zeppelin for a sober head now instead.

Five July

Along the curb where asphalt meets concrete,
bridging the crack, a flattened snake of pitch
crawls, an ill-conceived trope stretching up and
down the street in this early morning heat
each inch of which is without shade as we
face a sun that seems but some hundred feet
going nowhere if not here, and I bow
head and cap, apart from the fact ahead
is a find one could call phenomenon
just as easily: dimes, five, brilliant, some
kid must have dropped and then somehow forgot.
Luck and/or lie of the eye, they are what
much of the walk I had sought—the unearned,
no-frill metaphor, an afterimage
of the grand finale the night before,
pummeled as we were by bursts in clusters
quasar-like, more laser-like than white and
round—dimes alive in limelight, Lucifer's
subwoofer for accompaniment, and
the atmosphere pure cosmic theater
under the cover of the colors of
Valhalla without war, celebration
without clouds, heaven without surrender—
Xmas without December. Speechless for
years, I raise a cold glass of water like
Zinfandel and toast to old infidels.

The Correspondent

Ah, the entertainment value, Stupid,
Bozo hugging bimbo, though bonobos,
cousins of the chimp, most promiscuous
devils—without demons, even in their
environs, in their glass house with the whole
freaking human zoo right out their window—
get my vote. But I'm just a journalist.
Hubris is my beat. Pennsylvania
is the name of the street. Jaywalk in this
jungle and they pull your credential. Cross
King Kong and your sweet meat is ever so
lovely to excrete. Objectivity?
May whoever in the audience would
never succumb to such illusion come
on down. Savvy that suave is what every
producer can never get enough of,
Quasimodo, bimbo, or bonobo.
Reporters? Well, you've heard of Heisenberg.
Some say we play the chorus in the play.
They say that we—not his thing—foil the king.
Understand it's you who make or break news.
Viewers have to be there for the viewing.
Watch your watch and we kill the funeral.
XYZ (Examine your zipper). If
your zipper is down, no news is good news.
Zipped? You're not with the program. Deadbeat. Whacked.

Agnostic Radio

Agnostic Radio. Maybe there could
be commercials like HBO's got on
CBS, and Christian Radio would
devour late night spots. It could lend the
emergency broadcasting system's trill
fabulous new meaning. Somewhere, with time
gone by, angels might be ripping off their
headsets at the shrill memory of fear
inherent in a mindset that includes
Judgement Day. Instructed to stand by, to
keep their hands off the dial or—in a more
lavish era—the scan button, they knew
mothers would be separated from their
newborns, husbands from wives, that their lives would
officially be over before the
program manager administered pop
quizzes even, let alone returned to
regularly scheduled programming. Sow
seeds of doubt in sentient creatures so
traumatized, and souls will sprout where are holes.
Under like circumstances the human
vole might not be angels' alien, but
with its own blind though visionary and
xenomorphic metaphysics of forms
yet see itself as beings before souls.
Zookeeper beware of tunnels in air.

September Ever After

A transparent tarp you use to haul leaves
belies the eyes, inflates, rises, a great
cape slung by wind over its back, as if
donned by some invisible enemy,
entity without shape. For the form of
fear is never Bear, never Ghost, never
Ghoul. Neither is it evil nor black of
hell. By flames or flashlight the mind still sees
inside the well, while fear's that . . . that thing that
jostles, even should you dwell in certain
knowledge of its presence, your prescience
laughable to the mouth of the hand whose
magic's hardly the glove on your jacket—
nor bite in your billfold—but a cold grip
on your heart. You awaken with a start:
Peace is apple pie without anthrax, the
quintessential mom's art, while you're outside
raking leaves and Dad's about to roll his
sleeves to adjust the carburetor and
timing. And while far more pastoral than
urban, Osama bin Laden's turban's
vacant the picture, which is not to say
war was then more pure, but that rather than
xanthic, leaves, when dervish-like they stood, spun,
yellow-red and blush-gold, in the face of
Zoids you stood, pretend sword in hand, deft, bold.

The Unsung

Among whole nations at this moment the
brewing of poets! Such assumes that time
contains our beginnings as well as ends,
Dear Universe, that verse be not merely
existential, more angst in a bottle
foaming at the mouth, sunk, on its way down,
ground, eventually, into more sand.
Heaven, on the other hand, is not found
in happy hour nor had for a song. Ask
John Berryman. While you're there, check out the
Kool-Aid stand where—hot damn!—the Jameses are
likely doing booming business, business
meaning not banking with Frank and Jessie
near and Wright and Dickey behind the bar.
O late, great connoisseurs of chaos, must
poetry plunge the best among us in
quixotic behavior while its savior
rests in songs of the unsung? Tomorrow's
seen it all already, it sometimes seems:
the public wants peacocks, wants exotic
uncles, wants suicidal aunts, the new
versions, when the poets only want to
double you over, dance the dance called the
Chiasmus, right your rites without reading
you the riot act or your rights. They want
zeugmas without mead, desire less need.

The Haves and Have Nots

Aye, even Shakespeare would plumb trade for my
bones. At this minute I gots a robin
crowing in clematis crawling up and
down my mailbox planted here at good ole
eleven-seventeen Robin Road you'd
figure patrons might wants to know, 'cause I
gots symmetry and I gots syllables.
Healf? I gots healf in a handbasket 'cause
I gots grandma's shawl 'cause I somehow gots
June pneumonia, gots antibiotics,
killer medicines, pills white as the doc's
light enough to spook hoarse out of horse barn.
Mrs. I gots too—nurse as well as wife.
Now tell me. Is I happy? Is I free?
On count one I gots poetry. On two—
poll the citizenry. Folks here'd sooner
quarantine creator than creation.
Religion? Heaven knows—if it ain't gots
swing, then I ain't gots a godblessed thing
to sing, so you knows I gots religion.
Understand this ain't just ink you read but
veracity come to dwell for all the
while in the sad city Felicity.
Xuthus, great grand chile of Prometheus,
yearns—even Will pines—for what I gots, by
Zeus, be it but birdsong in borrowed light.

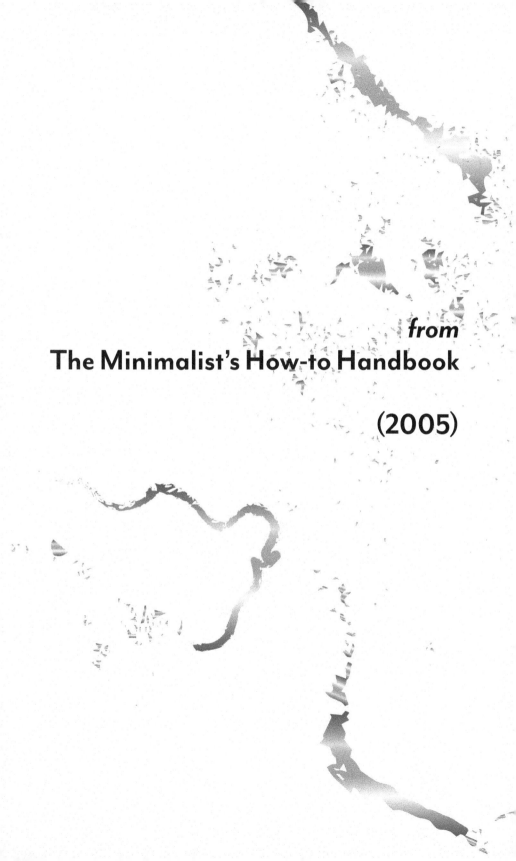

from
The Minimalist's How-to Handbook

(2005)

Alpha Images

A

In the beginning
God climbed Louis Zukofsky's
pocket step ladder.

B

We see from above
she faces east, her bosom
of the matriarch.

C

No great mystery,
he that rears on one hind leg.
Pegasus' hoof print.

D

Alfred Hitchcock as
pregnant with the devil as
with a certain air.

E

Where is the handle
and what hand stuck this pitchfork
into a snowbank?

F

Stand it on the moon
for a nation of ants, who
know not where they live.

G

Balancing a tray
with one hand, the other hand
poised to pluck the veil.

H

The minimalist's
gate to hell and heaven, these
corridors of light.

I

Blind to what's ahead,
behind, the ego takes this
pillar for a name.

J

Take pity on this
tattered parasol—too chic
for junk or joystick.

K

What looks like a squawk
is to the ear a moth or
butterfly, clinging.

L

Lest we should deny
the ethereal we have
the hypothenuse.

M

Dragging its belly,
a mechanical spider,
its nose to the ground.

N

A scene from Up North
on a postcard, a timber
frozen as it's felled.

O

The rim of the moon.
Peephole into an igloo.
Shadow of zero.

P

How you choose to hold
it determines the weapon.
You may need tweezers.

Q

Might this be the light
at the end of the tunnel,
the visible path?

R

Head, shoulders, and chest—
who's the cameo inside
this dressmaker's bust?

S

Suppose our hero
tore the spent fuse from the stick.
Say the sound of it.

T

Though you can't see what
road you're on, the sign ahead
reads like calvary.

U

More mind than matter
is symmetry's mirror. You
should be that lucky.

V

V is for virgin.
Whether spread or locked, her legs
are the point of view.

W

Symbol of tungsten
and the filament itself,
its light is the white.

X

North—as if a place
as much as idea—four
needles pointing there.

Y

This flower has bloomed,
become so huge as to dwarf
both stem and petals.

Z

Swordplay with air—zip
zip zip—stitches which seem a
bout to disappear.

Ciphers

1

Have you no shadow,
Adam without an Eve, O
thin man of Haddam?

2

Lest one doubt his feet
of clay, a reminder: this
beggar on his knees.

3

The unlocked handcuff
Houdini still sports, escaped
from the spirit world.

4

O cellist in midst
of a slow, low note—how still
your arm, string, and bow.

5

Surgeon's toy cannon,
radical vasectomy
or bad dream of one.

6

That swirling feeling,
once a sixth sense, innocence
sucked down the toilet.

7

The figure of one
sleepwalking. Little Zombie.
Baby Frankenstein.

8

Infinity Road,
the good Lord God's own address,
now closed to tourists.

9

Elephant—ear and
trunk—see it lean, laboring,
to best nothingness.

Logo Rhythms

+

Judas's cockeyed
kiss or sniper's four quartets—
hoarder's crucifix.

Check out the spoiler
on young Road Runner. Rootster?
Or rototiller.

∞

Complete with caption,
here is the cartoon for which
time wears its goggles.

∝

Open form; closed form—
which is which, these Siamese
twins whose names get switched.

∑

Some sure-fangled clamp:
certainty snakebit—though not
swallowed—jaws still hinged.

—

Ingot of lead or
of ink, entropy's ally,
plenty's enemy.

~

Ought one not doubt doubt,
a likeness caught here as if
an eyebrow, mirrored?

≅

What is turbulence
to one third is the bottom
of the flag unfurled.

=

Teeth tracks like ski tracks
in the white icing and/or
Oreo itself.

≠

Nothing is nothing
except when it's not something
that crosses the mind.

≡

Ichimi shizen.
Poetry and zen are one.
Shizen ichimi.

✕

The times you've sensed how
the straw through the lid might be
like sex with an ex.

‖

O pair of I's, you
who, covert captain, are true
to the rank and file.

⊥

Whenever heaven
plays croquet they borrow from
Euclid his mallet.

π

Bad ass attitude
in coat and hat. Stonehenge pimp
stroll in the abstract.

Δ

So then the voice found
Adam, said, You want I should
draw you a *picture*?

÷

Whose lagoon, what sky
is this reflection of the moon
and solar eclipse?

#

Your call: Italian
ticktacktoe or weighty case
of too much *vino*?

&

Am per *sand*? Even
the eldest of the monks must
have rice in his bowl.

%

Lest you look down on
the blind, know impunity
is a scent its own.

$

His serpent's tally,
Satan's monogram: Snake, one.
Adam? Love. Zilch. None.

The Minimalist's How-to Handbook

How to Write a How-to-Write Poem

First, write the title;
second, write the word *first*; third
write *write* — OK? Rest.

How to Mind Read

Close your eyes to see
an antenna rising there.
Follow instructions.

How to Levitate

Fasten the seat
belt of your chair. Sleep on a moon
smaller than your brain.

How to Read Aloud

Say to yourself though
you see the window you don't
glass. Words are the glass.

How to Eat Fire

Choose a brand with care.
The brand must not be longer
than your outstretched arm.

How to Walk on Water

Universities
don't hold classes on it. Try
a junior college.

How to Eat an Animal

Give it your dog's face.
Say you're sorry though hungry.
Now take up your fork.

How to Recant and Not Eat Crow

Your arm a lizard's
tongue, snag a low-flying crow.
Then let the crow go.

How to Live

Wild as it may be,
never say heel to your heart
lest you and heart part.

How to Have It All

It's very simple.
You don't have to be a monk.
It's not that simple.

How to Meet Your Maker

Think of a blind date
not unlike circumstances
when you were conceived.

Deus ex Machina: Six Chapters in the Education of Albert Einstein

The Wheel and Axle

The pure sensation
of an open umbrella
in hand, twirling it.

The Inclined Plane

As if whole oceans
were the rock of Sisyphus
rolling on the beach.

The Lever

What rimes with lover,
could cause the earth to move, whose
bearer talks softly.

The Wedge

The axe is a wedge.
Neither hands nor chicken necks
incur accidents.

The Screw

The original
spiral to hell—could it be
more simple? Baroque?

The Pulley

Would it were magic
and not squeaky wheels—the art
of levitation.

Demarcations

The Hyphen

Had you a whole line
of them you'd have your own train.
Imagine the freight.

The Colon

Eyes of a dead man
lying on his side, looking
into a bright light.

The Comma

Ah, giant embryo
with tail, what say you—yin or
yang, you little shrimp.

The Semicolon

A Spanish peanut,
a cashew—which's the best fit
for the appendix?

The Question Mark

Eerie character—
he whose lobe of an artist's
left ear is severed.

The Exclamation Point

Dah-dit. A signal
in Morse code turned on end: N,
you must solve for it.

The Period

How we've come to draw
with such sheer economy
the perfect circle.

Nocturnes

(Urania)

June, and in millions

       of jewel-like drops of dew

           dwell diminutive moons.

This is how heaven sends its scent

       so in the morning you

           use your hands to wash your face in it.

(Euterpe)

June, strewn white petals

       on the sidewalk cement

           where now splat raindrops,

a worn denomination of coin

       so thin there is only its luster—

           not the white of the white

but clear, an invisible thing distinct

       as the difference between looking at the yard light

           and at blossoms in its light.

(Clio)

June, and the boom of backyard fireworks

       like a tree that has suddenly bloomed

           on the horizon across town

has shocked the light out of the fireflies.

Now they travel more slowly, silently,

stupidly,

like the particles of darkness

they mostly are.

(Calliope)

June, and the juvenile great horned

is the sound of a rusty hinge

as the doors of its hunger open

at inexact intervals

on the solid geometry of the dark

where the parent owl waits

in silences long and several.

(Erato)

June, and with the speed of a hummingbird's wings

a bead beats the walls

of a plastic whistle

calling kids playing Kick the Can in.

The stars blink.

Doorbell lights link the houses in the dark.

Bedsprings, bedsprings, bedsprings.

All night

crickets sing.

(Terpsichore)

June, midnight.

The bugs have taken their last bite.

A neighbor's compressor

metallic as the cricket

shudders and falls asleep.

Parked under the streetlight,

Shawn's black pickup still ticks.

There is reason his shadow is quiet.

Who in his right mind

bounces to bullfrogs

plucking their fat rubber bands?

(Polyhymnia)

June, a day begun when the goldfinch

skipped the length of the lane like a stone.

When mayflies danced in place,

an erratic whirl of electrons heated by the sun.

When the form of the oak, the ash, the linden

turned amorphous in the breeze.

When in the afternoon a lost squadron of geese

flew so low overhead

their wings whipped up sound

not unlike dimestore balsa-wood planes,

their rubber bands wound and released.

When the only sign of now, the night,

was crow, sitting warily but still for his portrait

on the ball of a flagpole—shadow lord of all,

at once magnifying and soaking up the light.

(Thalia)

June, a delicate rain.

You don't mean to look up her skirt,

but now as if afforded a periscope,

you slowly focus upon the asphalt

turning from drab to patent leather.

(Melpomene)

June, and the funeral home lights

are on in the basement.

There has been an accident,

a little girl.

It is how the undertaker

will afford the hall

for his daughter's wedding.

Suppose in midst of preparation

he freezes, looks to the ceiling

as if standing under

the dumb thunder of a dance floor.

What love has joined

let not grief put asunder.

Should we take the bride's hand

to find the only step she knows

is the danse macabre, it is no wonder.

Why Elephants Scatter the Bones of Their Dead

1.

Having lived nose to the ground,
so to speak, then burial in thin air,
their scattered bones a metaphor
for their dissipated souls—
behavior as curious
as the trunk itself,
prehensile periscope,
forty thousand muscles
rolled into one
organ attached to a brain
so massive
as to be the envy of,
say, a Sherlock Holmes—
surely why elephants
are drawn to the bones
of even the outcasts
of their own kind.

2.

Flung, those bones must arc,
land in random patterns interlocking
and concentric, markers of the dead
and the realm of the living
and therefore the great domain
of the spirit of elephants
so the young need not stumble upon
nor fear death, shown the rite
of sowing the bones
of cow and rogue alike
to slowly grow more ghosts,
trunks become dumb trumpets
yet triumphant
as the quiet stride of an elephant
in this
or any other life.

3.
Or this is denial,
how the creature says
there's no such thing
as the vanishing elephant,
how collectively it rises,
a mote in gravity's eye—
feat
promised through its genes,
to be scattered always
as it also has scattered—
ivory the only remnant
of the elephants' graveyard,
scattered everywhere,
disappearing
before our very eyes.

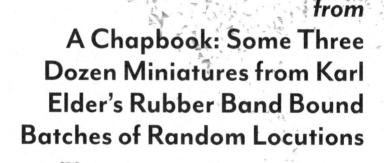

from
A Chapbook: Some Three
Dozen Miniatures from Karl
Elder's Rubber Band Bound
Batches of Random Locutions

(2007)

Auspicious Beginnings

I wanted to be
carver of pumpkins, forming
their flickering thoughts.

A Marriage

I snap a spider
in the ass with a towel
with precision, skill.

Whatchamacallit

You know, that name Eve
had for you now forgotten—
Whatchamacallit.

Mind like a Cave

What would I find there
but thought this dark as if scrawled
on the skull's far wall.

The Coal Bin

You could smell the breath
of Satan down there with each
shovelful of teeth.

Flagsong

Gravity defied,
that flutter and snap—measures
of wind that fly by.

Winter Joggers

The apparitions
of scarves in a blue breeze:
men trailed by their lungs.

The Art of Poetry

Some crayons are fine.
Make it a monster, compact.
Some stay in the lines.

The Art of Teaching

Hands behind your back,
bend forward at the waist and
pick up the apple.

The Ripe Cantaloupe

Its spot on top that
like an infant's cranium's
perfect for the thumb.

Factory

Not quite Einstein's spine,
still, this smokestack spews huge hair
on a churning brain.

Standing on the Pond Where a Boy Drowned

Mirror made of ice,
black, thick. Startled by my mask,
I look away quick.

God and the Great Horned Owl

Who else's straight man's
dummy swivels its head to
knowingly wise off?

Mirror in an Empty Room

Think of it as space
apart, the same space were it
the picture of it.

Waking to a Telephone

Shrill, electric strings
of pearls come unstrung, dropped at
exact intervals.

Existentialism

You're told there's a plan
in God's breast pocket. Your job,
then, is to pick it.

Getting Ready for Work

I wave goodbye out
the window of my mirror.
We should keep in touch.

The Telephone Poles of Kansas

Infinity's chain
gang, each figure bears its stark
cross of emptiness.

Dust

Just must they who would
trace their names in it become
the captives of it.

Playing Myself

The costume, gestures,
voice—each was easy. If I
just could get the lines.

The Art of Poetry II.

Wear Adam's death mask
to Apollo's masquerade.
Dance with each daughter.

The Art of Teaching II.

Hands bound and apple
held tightly in your mouth, now you
are all ears. Listen.

Vigil

Invisible now
the night: dark finally dim
as this moonlit room.

Sleeping Under the Stars

The meteors like
sperm trying to fertilize
the egg of the earth.

A Stockpile of Coal

So here's the devil's
cache, black diamonds in the rough.
You'd think he'd enough.

Where There's Smoke

Were the proverb wrong,
were there not always fire, must
nothing be ghosts' ghost?

Vacant Lot with Sunflower

His flock of clover
like wayward sheep, the shepherd
stands his watch, asleep.

A Vanishing

Why any sadness
in the razed barn with its space
risen in its place?

Illinois

No trees for miles
but this bare, fat, fence row oak—
the corn's religion.

Sasquatch at Sundown

All legs and small head—
my shadow looking back mid
stride at something said.

from
Gilgamesh at the Bellagio

(2007)

Gilgamesh at the Bellagio

O, it turns out the sonofabitch and
narcissist is immortal after all—
epicure, of late, at faux Lake Como,

The Bellagio, where his spirit reigns,
where fireworks in rain of fountains flower
on the half hour to tunes feigned by the moon;

third he is if body and mind are thirds,
his air of arrogance apparent as
are we, his subjects here in a manner
equal to air's a phononym of heir,
equivocal as the hole in our "O"

for what, opposite, looms tall, erect, lit
over the shoulder—no evening, it, in
Uruk or Paris—mock Eiffel Tower,
ready, poised to prick its floating ovum.

Freudian perhaps? Hardly erotic.
Indicative of an imperative
vying for the right of reproduction,
élan if élan's Elvis in the round.

Seen, read assbackwards, the scene is civil.
Indeed, denuded, devils spell evils.
X—leave it, Enkidu. Dude's an asshole.

So where to from here for pure, ascendant
entertainment? Helicopter flight to
violate the only virgin in sight?
Exciting as it might seem, why dream when
Neverland is now, our own Grand Canyon?

Enkidu, dude, we'll do the strip, do her
in her innocence, her ambiance of
giant light. Tomorrow. But not tonight.
Hot damn! we blink. To think—the only scheme
this bunch had for brunch was a Krispy Kreme,

no protean flash in pan to be gleaned
in neon panoramas paned by foot
(no fleet feat, given how far apart art
eats). Whether, Paul Bunyan, thy bow-legged

thighs were as wide as the St. Louis arch,
even were our Babe the sky, they would, could
not match the stride of Gilgamesh—hollow,

enormous with hunger—thrust and no gait.
Lust like this, we trust, must have purpose, must
enter the arena with more than its
vision to vamp us. Let's hubba-hubba,
Enkidu. It's your turn to test your luck,
now, on your own Humbaba. You'll need coin,

time, which there's such scarcity of, and un-
wavering love. Of what? is the question;
err we with answer is to shun the quest.
Love of the test itself? Of itself, love?
Variety's Old Spice, vice? May it be
endgame—no draw, no mate. Should we pocket

the eight by accident or intent, there's
heck to pay—no stroke (backspin, massé or
impeccable English) that circumvents
reticence enough, the cost of gain loss,
those slots sluts that, despite sloth, take their cut,
eschewing the lot of us by at first
enticing us with the thinnest slice of
nonplus pie to reject us like a slug.

Foray for us is we know the plot, can
obviate sure fate, unlike the brides of
Uruk—who knows if they faked it?—lithely
reclining to take it, let alone grooms
that cowered like whipped pups and to whom on
each's tomb, we are left to imagine,
each's widow might have chiseled, "One can
not / omelet con- / coct with chick- / en guano."

F you, too, Gilgamesh, sire of bastards
incarnate, though we are your brothers, blue.
Fuck Humbaba and Bull of Heaven, too.
That's it, Enkidu, yes, that's the spirit—
Eat your own feces, bark at your own moon—
Enkidu, dude, stop. Your point's well taken:
no more dreams for Enkidu. You don't owe

shit when The Shit owes you. So the mind says.
In the real world, though, body sides with soul,
ex animo. So let us go. Forego
this schism which is, in truth, illusion—
ego, id, superego. Thus it is—
edict: we live. As for identity,
neocortex is more vortex than crown

such that dull halo and dim bulb aura
ever follow in tow—the id the lead
vehicle flanked by superego and
ego. Semen delivery system?
No, like a metaphysical dildo
that points back to the Bellagio, we
entreat the gods of opulence, of
elegance, fortune, and gastronomy.
Not to preclude circumambulation.

Every rounder knows: you do Vegas, that's
inescapably what you do—you cruise.
Gambling's one ambit; the grandest gambit's
had at the Bellagio, Gil tells us,
that while he prefers goggles, we ought to
employ (nary need to spike our cocktails)
each, our glasses, the waitresses' asses
nicest in town—not an augmented orb,

no, not one, to be found. It's the real deal
in the flesh, those floatation devices
nestled up front, signal in a slit if
ever libido saw it, enough to
turn id into drooling idiot or
eddy of adolescence—the desert's
ebb, Little Gilgamesh, as it, throbbing,
now twists in Gilgamesh's fist, an o

the lips on that fish id ogles as chub
woggles under grasp at our gasp, Gil bent
entirely at the waist, wrapped in rapture.
Neither quite autoeroticism,
this, nor, exactly—hand mirror in hand—
your typical gaze into your navel,

the boy, our man Gilgamesh, has a thing
with mother, the Uber-mother, whose name,
Eternity, is written here in great
numbers and which, it turns out, our guy G
theorizes is encrypted among
Yea, the waters, Dude. This is no brachi-
opod, no fossil, this Gilgamesh, whose
nautical prowess, now more prowl than prow,
eludes all scrutiny as we circle

the convivial cove, mounting stairs to
where atop is the moving sidewalk
expediting all suckers and souls, though
not all are tyros who would enter here—
the sharks chauffeured to this revolving door.
Yea, touters among you, the most compe-
tent of Lucifer's legion, cut, run. Make
way, for here wades Leviathan whose heart's
object's no gambol or gamble. Blue chips

the weight of which could cause the earth to pitch
will not detour him from appointed rounds.
Enkidu. Dude. Wait. There is that we must
now get straight. Eden's tunnel's run's too deep,
too snug to turn back from. Yes, Dude, this means
you. Just as Eve's desire has capaci-
ty to assume a pleasing shape, we are
he as you are me and we are all_____—hint:
rhyme it with feather or plucked. Let it fly,
Enkidu; fill in the blank before time
escapes, twenty-three skidoo, from view. So

this is where thirst drives us—no more stalking;
water awaits our pilgrimage, the mind
enmeshed as if by body stocking. Hence,
none sense this fishy face, largess to dodge
the doorman who, unawares with muffled
yawn, nets not just guests alone but the in-
famous, incognito G, the great catch
of the ages. Luck's a trade, line of the
unlucky—blind, dumb, then gone. It's a wash,
rebirth. To play the game of some zero.

Theosophy, this? Or antithesis?
Would it were enough to backfloat the flow,
ease-by the ubiquitous, bloated B's.
No. The hobby we could have gazing at
the lobby's florid ceiling (in spite of
yowls from yon craps tables and bars), a girl-
friend, or two, or three, we could per chance meet,
infatuate, escort, promenade to
virtue or liars' lair—whatever. Or
even skirt it all, traipse counterclockwise

to time and space ante-Cirque du Soleil
when/where Picasso meant energy—not
entropy's eatery, its menu chic,
nauseating, bazaar of the bizarre,
tripe like "Snake Xerophilous sans Cactus."
Yes, Gilgamesh, the serpent's us, Narcis-
sus under glass, coiled, gluttonous gut of
incubus, icon of decadence, the
xenophile possessed by the zodiac.

Enter we now the inner sanctum, Sir
Penance's own vault and penthouse, the most
improbable of grottos, where our shrine
languidly swallows its tail in the form
of tall, perpetual, chocolate falls.
Gone black are the B's bay windows that look
upon tomorrow, pools where we shall lean,
eye the nothing that is our reflection.

The Be and the End-All

Z ain't just for zabecedarium,
yo mama know, be it a bumblebee's
ecstasy or disappearing ink she
wrote on yo memory, sparklers in the
velvet dark when y'all was but a chile still
unda the spell of her simple magic,
that brand that conjured a bee figin to
see to its deft deed, while in no big-ass
rush to think on its ownself when it's gone
(queen rightly a drone's supreme being), e-
pistemology only fuzzed-up buzz
of what was once adroit ontology.
Now, y'all sees being's alter ego: N
made to lie on its side or, say, the side-
lines where it come to has its lazy ass,
K.O.'d, tackled far shy of the end zone,
jersey ripped all to shit, though you O.K.—
intact, Jack, dude back from bed to mend his
head with vinegar 'n brown paper 'n
good to go, albeit a bit dizzy,
focused on the buzz, that hive alive as
Eden in autumn. Or is you dense, plumb
dumb, sos neva to sense the true human
condition: that hum inside yo helmet,
Boy, ain't hell a'tall till fizzled bulb, Bub,
a noise like sparks snuffed in the starless dark.

American Bovary (The Cosmetician)

Zip code sans abode: for one, one won one
yet lost all heart in Cleveland, where Madam
X, one's spouse, made it big to then make off
with a dollhouse manufacturer from
Versailles. "Forsooth," her lover crooned to her,
"you learn how false true love when you face the
truth," truth being the manufacturer
sooner than later would fracture his skull,
ramming headboard to topple wall, crying,
"Qui vive!" over his living doll, her rouge
powdered-plump cheeks, those coarse, horsehair lashes
open suddenly, as up she rose, too
nonchalant just for lust, but wantonness
more blind than a pair of glass eyes combined.
Looking down, she loathes her frog prince's drool,
kit, and caboodle; knows she ought haul tail,
jiggle and cleavage, to Cleveland; recant
in grand style to an emasculated
husband; then don her own wand for love of
green bred of her black magic, instead of
funds bled pure white, the spit and miss of spite.
Economics masked in histrionics,
dogged with life in a mirror, poodle turns
cat staring back as if groomed to scratch the
bitch, her itch gone south, home, to her own kind
a la KY, where, for one, one ate one.

Love in the Time of Quantum Mechanics

Zircon cons, but not even a pendant
yea long cons like a diamond—Sax or Brand
X—carbon hardly being forever.
Water, more genuinely speaking, is—
vaporized ice. Hold a glass to the light.
You shall possess insight, shall partake of
the spirit world of diamonds, two rungs of
separation from the nether world of
raucousness that is the nesting grounds of
quarks, of squarks, of leptons, of sleptons, of
photons. Photinos? Photons you've seen. Say
"Hola" a Los Photinos, new to the
neighborhood. It's no surprise that with a
million million million atoms known to
live in a teaspoon of water there are
Kilkenny cats, that quarks are quirky, that
just as there are sleepers there are leapers.
It's the whang on Yang that makes for the squarks.
Here he lies in the oral embrace of
good time Yin, the marriage's darker half,
for which its design is homologous,
each of two embryonic states of grace,
deaf to our deft imaginings: Is this
cosmology or numerology?
Be it two, three, four dimensions or ten
a cosmos of sparticles is no gem.

American Masque

"Zodiacal light," I write, blot from thought
"y" in Why. Why, slowly surfaces par
excellance a picture of sound of it:
Wh—faint though sonorous trace of Luke and
Vader, florescent hum from their sabers
under a neon horizon. Listen,
the year is 1977.
Star Wars has just been released, is all the
rage. Take radio waves like W-
QRS of riot-roped Detroit: to
pump pomp among soul and pop (classical
or romantic) seems just the ticket for
negrophobes who've flooded the suburbs, as
much as for the brothas, who stays back to
learn—canna Colt 45 in dis hand,
Kool in the otha—how you earns respek,
Jack, some serious dignity, Blood: dude
in the voice of a bad ass James Earl Jones.
Hoist a toast to you unholiest of
ghosts and whatchu gotschu's an Oreo
for an aria—stale one at dat, dat
ever chile (man and girl) unnastands ya'll
doff dat Nazi hat and mask—shore nuf dat
cat ain't but a double dosa ugly,
Bigga's cat, ghastly white black rat cat. Juz
ax Mrs. Dalton's cataracts, Bo. Shit!

Acme Academy of the University of Megalomania at Melancholy

Zeno, stoic before there were Stoics,
your colonnade calls, whereupon I scrawl
Xs and Os in the dust as if hugs
Were smug gestures at odds with kisses, where
verily you spake unto me, "Howbout
you play yourself a little tic-tac-toe,
the aim to outwait fate?" Or am I all
screwed up, confusing you with that other
rogue from antiquity by the same name,
quorum in this phantom forum of bum
philosophers: novice less paper, the
old boy in back honing scissors, and you,
neo-Zeno, the rock. Moreover, I
must bring to pass the task without ink, must
lilt like doves, while one's double, the soul, is
keelhauled through heck on the senses and back,
jolted dead awake to your namesake's odd
intent upon a rapt paradox of
halving one from illusions of many,
God having flunked Intro to Anthro, the
first twist in this, His less-than-orthodox
enlightenment foisted upon us, His
dark little tryst away from home when it's
common sense He ought to return where He
belongs—no harum-scarum harem of
angels to pluck, "He loves me . . . loves me not."

Divine Comedies

Zany's the name on a tongue gone amuck—
"Yeti," as if a sixth brother Marx barks,
expels its syllables in sixty-fourths
which, stuttered, turns the air rubber, Mel Blanc's
voice's inimitable ode haunting
us as when into the crevasse Goofy
trips and up from the abyss rises that
slick, primordial yodel of pure fright
reserved for flight with streaming ears for wings.
"Quit," begs the tickle-ees of tickle-er,
pneumatology and aeronautics
of angels aside, while in all truth it's
not less feathers here sought but desire for
more. Are not among the masters of the
last century those who scat its effects—
kaleidosconic their Calliopes?
Jazz in the form of joules, shards of stained glass
in the ears of cubists do not suppress
honed, hopeless groans of the dubbed, that stupid
Godforsaken look and plea, the Elmer
Fudds, the Daffy Ducks, Bullwinkles, Goofys—
every sorry citizen whoever,
duped, would think himself free, now "twapped by a
cwazy contaminated wabbit" that
breathes hilarity with hell's own bellows.
Abominable? Just jokes. That's all. Folks.

Professor Lucifer in the Arena of Angels

". . . zooplasty on a grand scale, Uncle's
yen to adorn the soul with sense beyond
Xs sewn for eyes on sock dolls (Jacko's
watch, no parallax in that lax, cross-eyed
vision: sight sans insight, its dazzled look
under scrutiny), hence, mind, rather, how
the mind, being an appendage to the
soul, is in the scheme of things meat met with
raison d'être for a treat, then the barbe-
cue where for desert there shall be apple
pie flown back from Eden, a rare entrée
of undetermined fare preceded by
none other than a gangrene salad, a
much-maligned primordial soup, and, at
last, appetizers beneath a spell of
knelling, metaphysical handbells—no
jumbo tolls, no subliminal signal
invoking a horde of winged dogs to the
hunt. O, my incalculable lovelies,
gods of the loft that in such myriad
forms are but air, stacked vapor, and old light
everywhere but where you are, which of you—
deaf ears, hollow eyes, numb tongues, and no thumbs—
can tell me whereabouts besides the foul
bowels I shall make the incision, what
angle take to free from flesh the angel?"

Zucchini Surprise

Zucchini Surprise, that original
yummy remembered much more for its size,
ex post facto takes the cakes, lights the lights,
wins ribbons, is gobbled now as the prize.
Voluminous, hence, are the almanacs.
Ubiquitous, therefore, is the seed, for
this is the future, time of hunger and
starvation to make potato famines
resemble hell's hiatus or the Queen's
quay. Cockroaches, entomologists say,
part and parcel, shall inherit the earth.
O so why should one not assume there'll come
no dearth of dirt, when the cockroach also
must eat, asks the last eugenicist, who
loves a twist, dreams of zucchini like a
king cobra to hiss and spit, scare the be
Jesus out of it—the cockroach, that is—
instead of—before the bombs—a mongoose.
Had hell no hunger would it still be hell?
Go figure: to take away one leaves none.
For the final feast there shall be, at most,
each an eater and eaten, then, at least,
defecation, if not defecator.
Child of Kafka, imagine: in an old
bed of manure the cockroach awoke
and found himself to be a zucchini.

Less Is More

"Zabwino," they say in Chichewa (no
yokemate to English, its alphabet sans
X), translated as "good things will happen,"
which my tutor utters with such faith, such
verve, I flinch with pure pecuniary
umbrage at his steep charity, as he
trades a priceless word for a two bit phrase
so—praise all blessings—I in turn read how
rich would be a world for which the play in
Q & A's without question answer to
problems unplumbed by an alphabet with-
out not only an X—but a Q, too.
Nudged to weigh anew, I sense twenty-six
minus X & Q's more than twenty-four,
leave door ajar on the lid of this I-
kid-ye-not, fixed, ready-mix metaphor
jamb-packed where the abstract meets the concrete.
Eye to eye, I ask Alistarico
how then in Chichewa one says *question*
(green again, the tongue tastes fun), so he goes,
"Funso." "Say what?" I say. He says, "Funso."
Ever so slowly the o on his lips
deflates as though through a closing hatch I
see a ladder he now retracts, heading
back, while I'm left to man the moon—wise guy
all agog—cross my heart and trope to vie.

A Routine Physical

"Zomax," she reads aloud, the student nurse,
"You're still allergic to it?" That's one R-
x they axed, I nearly blurt back, tongue still
wringing itself dry of wrath, bathed in the
vile, mild bile of impatience. Of course I
understand that she asks. One must play act
to earn license to practice, just as I've
sat, cool and fuming, relearning how to
relax, waiting my turn, chalked against mis-
cue of memory. "It killed a bunch of
people," I softly say. "Oh?" she goes, bent
on my chart, busy with her own business.
"Noxious stuff, Zomax. They took it off the
market before you were born." Now her head
lifts, her eyelids with it. "Ah," she says with
ken, yet the curiosity of Doc's
jar of Popsicle sticks, so that just then
is the moment—as she raises her watch,
having reached for my pulse—for which I so
gently take in my right hand her left wrist
for reasons I don't understand until
even she seems to see it: how close rose
death's old ghost on the drive here, heat ahead
coming off the pavement, invisible
bees swarming in hives of air and white light.
"Eh . . . ," I say, "no rush. The good Doc will wait."

Snapshots

Zzazzip. Old Gladhappy here. Another
year. A window on the Thanatopsis
Express and you the engineer with a
whistle, a party favor, its zzazzip.
"Vamoos," you spit at the photographer
until photographer gets the picture:
the cowcatcher's on the caboose, the train's
stopped, this shot of you with the look of a
Ray Carver under the weather, on the
q.t. about where you're coming from (the
pane of a phone booth?). What's there but to dial
O, though slow to do so, to disclose woe
no noble plotter ought to opt to pose;
moreover, was it not John Gardner who
laments, Sure death for the poet is to
keep the wound closed? Chivas in one hand, Georg
Jensen briar in the other, there you are
incarnate, austere, Sir Carver Gardner.
Holy steak and cake! Holy omnivore!
Great green gobs of greasy, grimy gopher!
For what? For the gusto? Or for "it," what-
ever it is sits in the gut so low,
drives you to chug and smoke, and causes the
camera to capture by missing it—point
being the point of being's not to quit,
addict of the rush in hissing, "Screw it."

Shining

for Joanne Lowery

Zapped in the back with a Rayovac beam's
yards of teeming mist, this live planetoid
X (that might as well be light years from us)
wedged in a fork of paper birch (inert
victim of blind, benign voyeurism,
unfazed by the likes of us low-lifes) lies
the cub porcupine, whose guise at dusk, a
scrub brush turned up (sans any chance in a
race from us, tortoise, or tamest of lame
quadrupeds), but with a gorgeous hue of
pewter so rare as to be the sheer form
of itself that (in urgent fervor to
name in order to more perfectly re-
member) a Plato might call angelware—
light the gown angels wear, their gossamer
karma aura's alloy in the ideal—
jerry built, as is always the human
idea of the beautiful, when our
history has yet to happen on some
godforsaken, lopsided moon on the
far edge of the farthest galaxy, where
eons from now sparsest particles rain
down in a mist of emptiness here sensed,
coveting the porcupine's seeming o-
bliviousness to angst and bliss alike,
as hid in its caterpillar crawl—wings.

A Disappearing Act

Zowie, word in a hummingbird heard—gone.
"Yikes!"—what it seems to say with its lofty
exit, its scaredy cat, peek-a-boo play.
We the peephole to hell, perhaps, remain
virginal in terms of maiden flight to
unparalleled heights, but on unchaste chase
to unearth heaven here, I say, "Holy
scat, no angel if not Tinkerbell's soul
rates wings like those." Still, should time come for res-
cue—fire or ice—would I kowtow? Does the
pope in his garden clamor for ladder
overhead, that bee-line and blur in the
noise of the hummingbird, thin rope of hope
more like from a toy helicopter and
less a flying saucer? I don't think so.
Kaput means kibosh, ash for balderdash,
je ne sais pas. Dares one stare dead in the
eye of the beholder seeking beauty
here with a mirror, or does one shudder,
gnostic who pictures black behind the glass?
For fortitude—out of fortune, fear or
egress—is faint ally to existence,
dawn the round nemesis of time's eclipse,
cyclical as it is, as is the coy
buzz, the quick charge, the discrete retreat of
all muse, that, game won, song sung, vanishes.

from
The Houdini Monologues

(2010)

[The Word]

You remember, Wife, the word, the word
that when you heard it Halloween, it would be me talking
and not some pseudo-swami shaking the table.

Well, here I am, on the verge of mouthing the word
for the umpteenth time, though I know full well
that around here the atmosphere is so thin
that to say the word is tantamount to
blowing on a dog whistle.

Not to mean I ever thought of you as a b.
Or me your master.

You remember the word is the identical word
that is an anagram for the nonperson
I'd ring for, station to station,
to let you know when I'd taken the show on the road
I'd made it ok.

Remember, you'd say, "Operator, he's not here."

Wife, I cannot count the times the word has fallen
on deaf ears, the phones all white in this upscale hotel
like in the movies. You do remember the movies—right?

Each time I lift one of the receivers,
house phones here, the operator speaks in such a whisper
as to be behind the range of mountains
and out of range, cloud mountains, that is.

 I suspect you must go through her to reach me.
At your next séance, Dear, think hard
of our word, gazing into the crystal.

Say the word, Wife. Embed it in a message
even must it remain an enigma, lest there come a time
you cannot recall it. I remember it.
I only wish I could forget the bloody thing,

trade it for the memory of your name.

[Pie in the Sky]

I'll take a table near the window,
my back to a wall of deep, fabular blue.

My waitress will wear a sheer apron
and as she feigns scratching my order
she will do so with a stub of pencil
you can see there is no lead left.

Because I am a regular ·
we need not speak. Stormy or mild
she sees through me,
as I see through her,

as I see through the table top
through the menu to my shoes,
which look like howling holes,
unlike her shoes,
which are Cinderella's slippers.

Later, before she pours me coffee
it will sit in my imagination
like something missing,
weak but steaming, perhaps,
as the weakest tea steams
like water.

When I go to reach for my fork
somehow she will have forgotten it.

How now to get her attention?

My mouth waters so over thought
of tons of whipped cream on my tongue
I would sound like a drowned foghorn
and she'd never find me.

I should slip out of here.

I should leave her something to,
next time, insure promptness.

[Earthscape]

What, for sake of inspiration, for respite
in midst of the solitude of the absolute,
does the soul do? Understand this: Fossils, say,
upon which one focuses
for the fun of it, for their beauty,
to see in them patterns like hoarfrost on a window,
like ferns, like veins in a leaf or purple on a leg—
these are prototypes for the only art that hangs here, Earth's surface,
and you shall come to know it as you've known the seasons.

Who's the fool who says all life's an illusion?
I tell you look into your palm!
There you shall view your future—
all the roots, the flames, the Chinese dragons,
abstract expressionism, spinal columns, bas-relief,
shadows of the clouds like birth marks that move.

Art—it comes and goes as the clouds come and go.

[Vocation]

A perk, magic I never dreamed of
on the other side,
is the capacity of the human soul,
without the distraction of the body,
to ascend at will to a higher plane of thought
with what I imagine is the forgotten sensation,
is the resistance then sudden click in the hand
of the on/off knob of a solidly built radio.

What I'm trying to tell you, Dear—if by some
miracle heaven should allow that on these innumerable
streets we should meet—
there are air waves with uninterrupted,
indeed presumably eternal,
music.
But no news.
No casualty reports.
No forecasts.
No Jack Benny.
Not even a jingle.

Then, again,
perhaps it's not music at all
but the air waves themselves,
of the thinnest sort,
of the wings of insects,
no-see-ums.

Something is telling me I ought to have repaired
radios for a living, like the one that stood in our parlor.
I could have had a hobby shop instead of a library.

I can see it now, looking down upon
the uptown of some megalopolis
impossible to identify with the cloud cover.
Still, the skyscrapers are not unlike the silver
and glass tubes visible through the back of that radio of ours
such that when, once, I went
to replace a tube,
I could not tell which of two futures
I mused upon—
a miniature utopia
or this moment.

[Psalm: The Persistence of Light]

You know the moment
when on the horizon
you've mistaken distant clouds for purple mountains
and for an instant
you know where you are
and you don't
as in dreams you know where you are
and you don't
and the light
it's not like in the Bible or any book
but shape without dimension
like the sphere
you now think about
containing the same clarity
that is the thought containing it
that does not roil or billow
clarity that is to air
what air is to space
curved as light is curved
which the eye won't have but eyes it straight
as when the mountains disappear
yet they come back
as the clouds and the light
they come back

[Metaphysical Laryngitis]

You do not know what silence is until you say it.
There's a new fellow here, name of Cage.
Normally when one speaks a bubble appears,
something like cartoons with no caption.

Not this old boy. His is more of an echo
like the diminishing vista of a hand mirror
held square before a mirror
or memory of your best toss,
skipping stones.

I was so excited when I saw that that
I might have wet myself. (Then as now my gown's gauze
hints of albino asparagus.)

Yesterday (or what might be yesterday, there being
no night or day) I tried engaging Cage in conversation.
There was great clucking of tongues and words
that rose to the surface to burst into nothing
like talking to yourself under water.

If my mind was sheet music, his voice was nothing
but whole notes. I'd trade anything for that old feeling
of a key, instead of a bubble,
tucked up my you-know-what.

I'd say it with sign language but it's like I'm handcuffed.

[The Paucity of Unending Light]

With exception of your kiss,
less the key it sometimes contained,
of all things on Earth to miss,
that which I miss most is mirrors.

All of the light of heaven I'm here to tell you
is a mirror to a blind man.

So I dream of a haberdashery, a man
across from himself before a folding triptych of mirrors
in—instead of a straightjacket—a tux,
the tailor over his shoulder without a face.

I think of your lipstick, your purse,
which held your compact,
but not before I think of its mirror,
which is no mirror until, unlike a music box,
I open it and it bears your imperfect portrait,
your absence—its perfect silence.

Open the medicine cabinet. Presto. You vanish.

It is only through a turned-down mirror, Dear,
you shall know the truth of here
and the unimaginable magic,
the divine beauty,
of there.

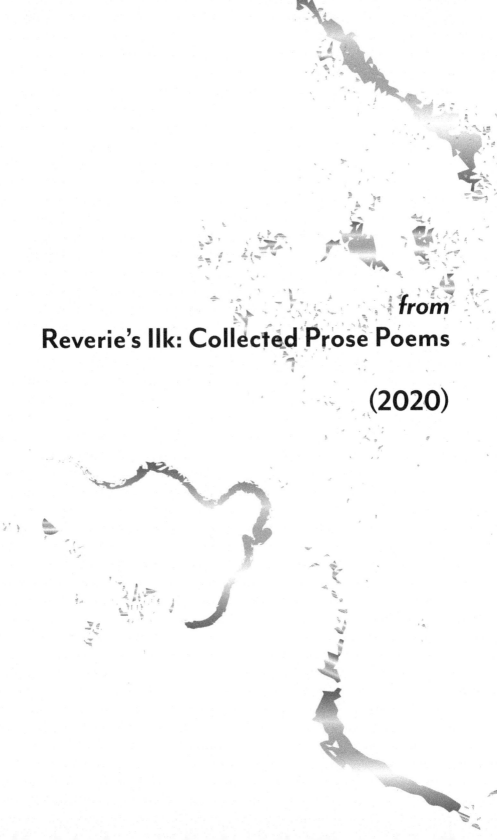

from

Reverie's Ilk: Collected Prose Poems

(2020)

Learning to Talk

There is another organ beside the tongue that does not scar. The brain. It is there among convolutions you had your most fluent dream of the bean you snuffed up a nostril at four where it took root.

Is it any wonder you stole the bean from your mother's pantry? Is there any doubt it is why on occasion, like a blind man, you think with your hand? Your fingers, they are tunnels for you to travel to depths you have not known but felt when, as a child, you'd be on your belly, burrowing with your entire arm beneath damp sand you'd made a mountain of.

Likewise there are mountains and caves you have made in the mind, airy vowels and dark consonants, as if language were made of words and not the urge they represent to go on talking, this inexplicable surge of energy from atoms and quarks that arrange themselves, here, instead of on some distant star, instead of where you are.

A Life

With both hands a small boy holds a ball of string so big it doesn't occur to him there are two ends, so far from him is the center. It is only after the string is tied to the kite, the ball growing smaller—yet, with each glance, more vivid—that he can predict a beginning, the nothing the sphere is wound around.

So it is that somewhere between boy and man he is made to understand that the atom, too, is hollow, and therefore the universe. He comes to see that this is how his life will go, that the string unwinding so fast, which at the very last he was unable to hold, had nothing to do with a beginning or an end, but—like the makings of the sphere—everything to do with both.

The Cockroach

Not tall enough to use the urinal in Union Station, my youngest settles on the third stall he inspects, relatively clean, until something he's not seen in his life chases him out, a cockroach to rival any I've met, mean as a mongoose I remember saying once in the Far East, so that Wade's shout won't scare it off, though shrill enough to stifle the snores behind the door of the next stall over. Later, of course, there are questions. Like why don't they mop the vomit. And why was that man sleeping in there. So I tell him.

And now a week later I want to take it back. Not that I lied. Or even told the truth. But as I watch him boldly swim for the first time just beneath the surface, as if to defy the net, his even bluer eyes open underwater, searching for my hands, and as I lift him slick, sputtering, wide-eyed, and for the moment bald, I look into his face, that Tweety Bird face absent its coyness.

Wade, what we saw that time on vacation when we got off the train. I wish it were not real-life. Just somebody's art with a capital "A." But that's not what I mean. What's important is I stamped my foot. The cockroach vanished. You, you went in there and you went. And that man. Why—when we didn't see so much as his face—did I make him out so low as to have a cockroach for a pet, as if a man who swims could not possibly drown. Let this be a lesson. I was the one not afraid, who now am.

Prepubescence

He was six when in the office he colored this big black keyhole on a blue Post-It and stuck it to the edge of a shelf. It's like a cartoon door on a dungeon without walls or windows. Sometimes I've moved it, unconsciously, hunting a book, yet a hundred times stood before a thing so stark it seemed there before he made it, what only a child could see to create, a reminder he can't be reminded of it, that for now there's no escape.

While She Is Away

The pipe is a sculptured meerschaum, and just as I sense she's about to ask, "What tobacco is that?" meaning "I like your cologne," I wield it from my teeth, yet balance it so quietly on the table that the bowl grows an endless strand of blue hair, so swiftly carried to the far side of perception, so very beautifully, I somehow know why love is a word I no longer need, and while my eye is fixed, she eases alongside me, slips my wrist and hand on like some elegant ornament, and places it, palm up, in my lap.

Sentiment

How can this be? Here I am, driving to Baskin-Robbins six months later, and for no reason I begin weeping uncontrollably for my molars—those crude, excavated pairs of dice whose numbers had finally come up. Their absence creates a real scene—my tongue darting from one hollow to the other, a new mother in search of her pups. "O Fate!" she cries, translating inhibition, rendering the loss in an image I can understand: stunted, bloody rooks toppled on the dentist's table as he shifts strategy, playing with himself on the hinged game board of my jaws. I stop the car. I shove it in reverse, determined to take a correspondence course, anything to gain knowledge of their whereabouts, the wisdom of another profession.

Jade Plant

She's calling me a dumb fart and yelling why didn't I unload the dishwasher and look at this shit smeared everywhere like the peanut butter on the counter as if this place were a goddamned sandwich or something, and I jump up and stomp over at her jade plant for reasons unbeknownst to me and bend over and go blah! blah! blah-blah! and it just sits there, green with envy, hundreds of fat, dumb tongues.

Bluegills

Were I to become a widower, I'd fish bluegills. The calm of early morning water'd remind me of this moment beside the sleeping Brenda. Her mind teems with a story told in the movement of her foot as much as her typing fingers—this spasm, that flutter felt in the taut line.

That's what's perfect about bluegills. The quick yet repeated mystery: not the catch nor its splash, but before, now, and always, the fish dumbly mouthing its hunger as if the story must be told through the dream of this woman—the story, I want to tell her, of my own.

The Elders

for Vicki and Dave

I.

This is our mother and father. They are not smiling, gazing here into the future. It is 1946. They cannot know they will have much to be happy about so they wear gray suits—she with a hat, with its hint of a veil and a corsage, he with a tie. Though he stares directly at us, his shoulder is turned toward her as if she holds his left hand in her lap, which we are not allowed to see. She, she is turned slightly to the southwest if behind them is due north. It is their wedding picture. You can tell there is affection between them but not for the world. She is thirty-three and he is forty. Each has been disappointed by love.

II.

Here is a full-length shot of Karl, our mother's father, slightly stooped, his fists jammed into his pants pockets to hold the tremors to a minimum. The sun is in his face, though he grins in our grandmother's flower garden through which he shuffles as if to ward off the Parkinson's. No one would know he's over six feet. Big ears and a protruding lower lip, he knows something we do not. Always. He chews White Owls and you cannot beat him at checkers. We will see him later in the basement of the First Methodist Church in Pittsfield, Illinois, standing behind a 50th wedding anniversary cake. He will be without open collar. Alta, whom he will not have been allowed to touch for the middle third of their marriage, will have dressed him. They will have, however, learned to love each other despite their anger. For the meantime he looks her right in the eye. He knows something, all right. He's always had her number. When we are kids we wear his cigar bands as though they are the insignia distinguishing us as agents of some mysterious order. In this overly exposed snapshot he wears his white hair. As one who knows, he is the White Owl. He will pass away with dignity, peacefully, in his sleep. His wife will be at his side.

III.

Now here we have Alta at seventy-five, still radiant, a studio portrait, of whom her son-in-law, our father, once said, "She's a high flying babe who never landed." You know by her smile she buys big presents but would wrestle a bum for a quarter. You can hear the choir from three blocks away when she's in town on a Sunday morning. She sang opera as a girl out of St. Louis when Karl, the grocer, snagged her off the tour. Therefore her God is song and entire congregations of Methodists have heard—if not seen—God. They think she is wonderful and so do we though they cannot possibly know the extent of our awe. When she came to live with us, a trial separation from her husband, she came to cook and clean. The house became the flower garden she left behind, the store, and the restaurant. How could our mother, with her father's temperament, match her? Our mother would listen. And listen. And listen. Her mother was her mother.

IV.

Meet Amos in a rare pose without Grace, taken perhaps in the basement of the same First Methodist Church to which Karl and Alta belonged. Amos owned the other business in town—Moorman's—having moved there off the farm for a better way of life in which there was time for the Bible, Zane Gray, his fellow Masons, and his wife, whom he would attend with the enthusiasm of a cabin boy and call "Kid" even into their eighties and who herself remained active in Eastern Star. He has the stern look of a man who will go far, having from so far away come, the deep lines in his face the mark of one destined for study, contemplation, and wisdom, while by day he tills a huge garden, makes wood, feeds the stove, and runs his bird dogs. He has the visage of a man who on the wall of his den there is an elephant gun. And there is.

V.

One needs not know her name to see the resemblance—this daughter of Providence. With an innocence that caused her to gasp in the midst of her "story," her soap opera, how she bore five children was a wonder. And that blond-red pair of halos wound and pinned above her head each morning, waist-length braids that once—visiting her house on a weekend, ready for bed—we got to unravel, help her brush twice one hundred. Absent from the portrait is her chair. Gone too to cedar chests are the elaborate doilies, the shawls, the sprawling white tablecloths she crocheted on her lap where she would lay the hook down in order to reach, to hold each face as we leaned, in turn, for a kiss. "How you wuz?" she would greet us, that playful chuckle as much an exclamation of how we had grown as it was a test of English. Grace, who as a young farm wife had an accident, who the last time she drove a car was her first, who "busted the barn door to boards," winked Amos, whose mutual love of language would have her, she of the faint heart, out of breath, as if he knew her soft laughter were her calisthenics. Now, three decades after her death, as if leaning into a Degas, a memory comes to surface. As circumstance would have it in that small house, a grandson burst in upon her dressing before her mirror, nude. I tell you the way she did not flinch was pure Grace.

The Spell

Finally, I drop to the sidewalk the stone I've held for a quarter hour or more, leaning at the edge of the Pigeon River bridge where at an angle below, maybe the distance from mound to home plate, a Great Blue Heron stands on the spill, a rock-and-driftwood dam, thanks to the abandoned labor of children. What luck I wear a T-shirt the shade of the heron's back! Or is it hunger that here trumps fear, as now, impossibly swift on her tucked neck, the pointed beak pivots east, toward a sun-blocked bank. Another minute. The neck uncoils into a backward question mark. Later, a dove explodes with a whistle from the brush to land in the rushes not six feet behind her head, and had I the heron's eye, I'd swear she did not blink. Then out of nowhere a second dove lands on higher ground, dump loads of rock white as chalk on the west bank. Even in midst of more flurry, even after the span it takes for the pair to mate, the question mark stays cocked. And that pose—such a taut yet specious emblem for curiosity, I think, caught as the heron is outside the net of human apprehension woven with a predilection for, say, film over a still photo, action over inaction, though with an inert point of view. As to her spell, it's no less in its lesson than the suspense: Before, at last, she vanished, banking behind cottonwood at the blunt-end bend in the river; before, quiet as a butterfly's glide, she flew low the length of the shaded corridor; before she rose, dangling legs trailing toes; before she embraced, hugely, the air in a flash of slowly expanding though sudden blue, there came at agonizing intervals the slightest, the entirely imperceptible extension of neck and attitude of bill until—quick as the spark in a patiently-wrought, dark haiku—the shot, the kill.

The Rock

This is a story of a man striking an unexpected rock in a garden he has worked for years, whether the garden is real or not. For a second he wants to look up to see his house is there, that he hasn't been plowing the neighbor's plot by mistake, but, certain this is no dream, he squats to extract the rock.

It won't budge. He shoves at it with his boot, but it won't be moved. He selects a lever and a concrete block from the shed. No matter how deep he probes there is more of the boulder.

Much later from a distance the gardener is seen with another man. They talk and gesture toward the ground. Each wears a straw hat. Both are leaning on shovels. Small mounds of clay contrast with the expanse of rich soil at their feet.

The next day the scene is so far away that the exhaust fumes from the backhoe are barely visible. There are more men now, standing in a great circle, staring down from the edge of the hole.

Nightfall. Everything is quiet. The yellow light from an aluminum awning upstairs cast on the green lawn like a single buttress remains on for an inordinately long time. At dawn a bulldozer arrives, fills the hole.

Again the scene is a close-up, the man is plowing around the rock that is the tip of an iceberg, the peak of an underground mountain, or the Earth itself—whatever. Only one thing is certain to the man: the rock is not of this world.

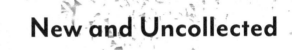

New and Uncollected

A Natural History of the Muse

Picture yourself one who uttered the first
time in the evolution of language,
"I can't believe my ears." Could it have been
your face that says what messengers are these
that the still wind now abounds in the form
of faint pairs of whispers, simultaneous,
thereby creating the cruel illusion
of harmony, of one world? Would the eyes
have been open to the possibility
that, alone, the mind is never alone,
subject to influence inside itself,
or might the eyes have darted from one ear
to the other in a covert display
of paranoia associated
with auditory hallucination,
not knowing that hearing frogs in winter,
say, is more common than seeing a ghost,
no matter what the season? These are strange
old questions even for a mind engaged
in psychoanalysis after it,
psychoanalysis, was invented.
Maybe there is sound reason when clichés
stir new found taste for the archetypal
as if of late they need not be mouthed to
be newly heard. Think of our prototype
showing its tongue, stopped in the middle of
whatever our prototype has begun,
when its ears, like the head of Janus or
Siamese twins endowed with a shared spine,
speak to each other of the world not with
words but as mirrors of insight, knowing
even where there is not sight, there is light.

Snowman

isn't
this
poem's
title, no,
just as this isn't
the brim
of his hat, just
as these aren't lumps
of coal but more like
cubes of sugar, just
as this is not a pipe.
Neither is this a scarf, nor
is this a red wheel barrow, no.
What this is is (a la Stevens) ink
on the back of an envelope—
or was, to be more exact,
before it was typed to be
emailed off at the speed of light
to become the absence of light before
it was rolled and tossed without the heft
of a snowball, which is not the truth, just as
this is snowballing toward a title below—
both visible and invisible like *like* without
the "k," like the buzz word for a buzzard
sitting on a blind man in a blizzard.

The Foreman and the Apprentice

For an instant you'd think it affection
that caused the man to grip your arm.
There you'd stand upon a plank before a bare
wall while something like a silent alarm
called all sensation inside of him, brow
clenched, wincing as if at a glimpse of hell.
He seemed not to want to talk about it,
nor for it had he a name. Another spell
is what we called it. And did not dwell.

How to say how sudden, how hard he shook
Without thinking madness or that he was ill?
He never missed a minute's work, nor took
time off, nor lingered on break. Lean, tough,
he'd slap the mortar down and lay another
block as if luck was all there was
and all there was was enough. Other
lives leaned on his—the guys on the crew,
wives, kids, and, not the least of whom, you.

The Lie

Never daring feed
the tall roan mare
fenced next door,
I saw without seeing
the look he wore
before he screamed—
my little brother, bit—
and grabbed the hand
to steal us past
the widower's porch
where suddenly
the old man stood,
yelling we were warned.

And I shouted lie,
cried the old man was mean,
called him dumb,
the only words I had
to say it wasn't fair
no one had explained
how terrible quiet
then loud could be pain,
and later wouldn't admit
I'd held my brother up,
mute as I remained
it wasn't the widower
nor his horse
that put us up to it,
yet how could my brother be
guilty of his fearlessness,
let alone me
my innocence?

Blanks

Yellowed yellow, this
formless flag of childhood
he drags through the house
as if—in place of dolls—
his collection were holes.

What stranger fate
for a bushel of cotton
than abuse through love
that while sleeping
or watching "Batman"
he will not be without.

Once, he volunteered
how to fold a corner,
to fashion a triangle,
holding it just right
to caress the palm,
because, he said softly,
he loves the touch.

And when on occasion
it becomes a cape,
I somehow think of Lear
and then schizophrenia
(the rags of madness
woven before we are born,
worn, sometimes shed or
worn again even to the end)
and know our lives as
the effect of self-love,
unrequited
except in the child.

Fog Noir

1.

Black, radiant,
reflected in still pools, puddles
the dog won't lap even when allowed,
a polish deep as a showroom Cadillac's
in shapes indistinct
as a cloud's silhouette—
shadows gutted of substance.

Should the walker see in that quiet water wind,
he ought to turn back. The very air
become rivulets of rain
here at his feet
or oil anointing all in its wake,
including the mind.

2.

Here even before
it arrives,
a sheer gauze, this fog is not so thick
you think of ripples the size of waves
in run-off caught in the ditch—
that slosh heard at once
by the dog and myself,
hardly Lock Ness
yet animal maybe
with an animal in its jaws.
The dog, seven months, has never known
such pain, straining at her leash. I,
meanwhile, merely notch another kill.

3.

Spring brings green things—
such was the prophecy of my son
who as a toddler called it
froggy outside instead of fog.
This morning in sun-baked fog
I counted a hundred frogs
squashed and belly-up on the blacktop.
The dog, herself a pup,

strangely ignores them all
as if to say of the phenomenon
she saw this in another life,
she smelled it coming.

4.

I stroll tonight not in celebration of fog
but the roller of big cigars,
as fine a philosopher as any lover
who knows life's great pleasures are all handmade,
sensing a vein in the leaf,
sensation rich as the scent itself
on a breeze intertwined
with a wind in Wisconsin
all the way from the Dominican.

I gnaw and puff, puff and spit
not into but with these gusts
behind us carrying the smoke
like renegade kites into April.
The juice. I like the splash and pattern
of it on the asphalt. It's the sound
of when we return home, and in a mound of old snow,
I stick the lit end, extinguishing it.
So what if I turn Republican.

5.

We leave streetlights behind, quick cross the bridge,
a new path at the edge of the village
past a lake made of rain
where, on the other side,
there's a barn.
Though harm's far from this fog
from which no evil could see to spring, we hide,
it seems, dog
and I, from a sound deep and low
like a foghorn about to have a cow
or slow, sonorous note a half-mile back from
Seth, whom we left home
practicing sax
she must ask, head cocked,
stopped
in her tracks.

6.

In midst of me transcribing all this,
Wade cannot sleep. Several times
I go to him behind the wall
behind this screen
to pat his back. Finally,
he knows what he needs.

I tell a story about the knight
the people couldn't tell from the dark
because of the fog
until the man who polished lenses
abandoned his craft for language. Thus
the invention of cloud,
that—like the knight and the dark—
one could see clearly
only by abandoning the realm—
Fog—
from which to escape
one walks toward.

Now, in the light of a dream
perhaps, he sleeps.

Outside
a week of fog persists,
as the dog sniffs,
sits beneath the quaking aspen—
each bud, though unawakened,
a leaf begun.

Late November Afternoon, Hazman's Field

"Who is the third who walks always beside you?"
What the Thunder Said

A man in gray overalls
steps out of the gray matter of the horizon.
Snow whirs above the stalks
like angels of locusts
to hush the wake of husks.
Discerning his face
is like trying to make substance
of atoms that won't adhere—
these flakes,
one of which, wafer-like
lights at your parted lips
like a hint of a name
partially quenching
the dry question of identity.
You freeze,
almost remembering;
something about another season,
person, and place.

April Upside-down

You dream you sleep beneath a sheet of sleet,
awaken, all perspiration, to find
what must have been the impetus of your
imaginings, as now you clutch the stair-
way rail, a startled glance straight up at sound:
that sting of flung sand hushed by clacks of clear
marbles, a brace of precipitation
punishing the skylight, as if to make
it understand, as you have understood:
out or in there's always weather; whether
you're asleep, awake, or but half aware
of who or what you are, you've learned your part
by heart: tomorrow, daggers drop—not off
of eaves-troughs only but onto solid
ground, under power lines, beneath the oaks,
and into the quick of whole moments, mo-
ments from which both past and future scatter
only to gather as past's sensed presence,
just as now is all there is to be known
of eternity: that cellophane sound
of the wind, of parted curtains of beads,
of fire in the clicking trees, as here and
there their sudden weight tears limb from limb
to leave the yellow marrow bare, hanging,
though one, an unusually large branch
on the lawn, is the reincarnation,
in abstract and absolute stasis,
of a prehistoric preying mantis
as it faces an unnatural foe,
unidentifiable, ominous
(once known as a mailbox), that should it turn,
wrenched, say, by the wind, pure grotesque, bearing
its bent, translucent, Pleistocene teeth, prayer
appears to be in order before prey
transforms to carnivore, catapulted
as you are to a time before Adam
where the clouds are waltzing angels,
where the high ceiling of their blue ballroom
is the floor of the orchard where you light
among rows of scores of cold chandeliers.

The Baffle

Feeder tray's husks
flutter and oft from fly
like the sparrows,
those flibbertigibits that,
quickened by snow and cold,
arrive in droves

while sporadically below,
tail a rippling question mark,
a squirrel forages, seeing not,
apparently, beyond reflection
in the window
the human in whom

there is no pleading,
no nose in the air,
no mock prayer
before this temple
atop a pole
shimmering, then still,

then another chill—this
winter of seemingly
eternal, external intervals—
as the bottom
of the stove pipe baffle,

the very edge
of its tunnel, funnels
the wind, rim
whipped in circles,
a wobbling

washing machine drum
in spin cycle at first
but more like at last
hoop on the hips
of a spry-as-a-spastic
spirit sprite.

Sunday Morning Run

Such fine light snow
like flour on dough
so that glancing back
at a dark track
enlivens the stride
as if to hide
the fact
of fat,
to appear
to be here
for fun,
communion
of one
with nature—albeit one's own.

Mile out of town,
a left, another, then down
the usual street
by luck to meet
the paperboy on his Schwin,
follow its trail so thin—
like a hair without end
under a lens—here a bend,
later a slit
in it,
taking on a turn,
looping in driveways to earn
delight
in its rhythm as might
a hymn
to Him
in heaven
or him in heaven
here, his presence certain,
seen in impressions so clearly human
as to be read
the rival of daily bread.

Angels' End

Can it be the wings are first to rot?
Why now this surprise when for twenty springs
you turn a familiar corner, never finding
in the shadow of the stop sign a fallen angel,
its soft but gritty carcass?

Though it's been a hard winter,
it must have been a massacre up top.
The dead in such great numbers
you've witnessed out windows of planes,
yet they were all lined up, ghosts reclining
in vague coffins, feather-white and buoyant
on a backdrop of purgatorial blue—
unlike the heap in the gravel lot across the street
that suggests forms never human,

though there's no comfort
even in the torsos of demon creatures,
let alone a mound like an albino sea lion
you earlier stumbled upon at home, tucked
along the foundation, out of the sun, out of sight.

Garbage Day in Howards Grove, U.S.A.

When on a morning walk
I'm struck by tons
of what some citizens think junk
stuck on the curb for pick up—
perfectly good flowerpots;
a mirror; rope
or cord, maybe,
in not impossible knots;
a blue sofa; stoves; one time
even a ticking clock;
and, once, with spines
that still cracked,
a complete encyclopedia
I later backed up
and hauled to my office—
I come across a trench,
a man swinging a pick in it,
and, since for a second
there seems to be none,
I give him purpose, rather,
fill the hole with purpose
as it becomes a tunnel
so on a Wednesday
so as the Earth turns
some of this pillage
might slide to another country,
a poor sister village,
and so the rest of the week
we could be pumped
all the nothing we need.

The Doomsayer

Omen of this poem, smoke
swirls out of nowhere, gathers
and descends like small tornadoes
inhaled at slow intervals
as if by a fire-eater without a brand.
As to the verse, may it
be more than a version
of your act in reverse,
behind the scene the stem of the pipe,
the bowl's interior,
which is cooling, growing
the tobacco and, in doing so, accepting
the smoke like so many genies back in a bottle,
transformed, trapped in their latent state
as a flame collapses into a match.
You are reminded of when there were wishes,
your only hope.
Drumroll.
The end is near.
And already here.

from **Leftovers**

Stove burner ticks like a bomb.

My watched pot—a saltwater lagoon.
Quart of navy beans
simmering on the bottom,
dormant as a bed of enormous clams.

Water and weather so clear,
I could drift here forever
if not for this hint of violence—
whisp of mare's tail on the surface;
husks nudging the sunken
tug of the ham bone;
then a couple of bubbles
as it creaks over on its side;
and then a bean,
a solitary bean
tumbling to the top like a cargo box.

The lid tolls.

Death by Chocolate

Sweet. Delicious. Deliberate.
Earned not in the conventional fashion
but from a carton
with an ice tea spoon
and a brand of ice cream
from a regional dairy in the heart of Wisconsin.

Contrary to what you may imagine,
the victim takes on
no new complexion, pallor,
nor pounds. The face remains
the body's face, surprised
should it catch a glimpse of itself
in the reflection of spoon
and not another self
in this slow death called
the life.

Yes, this is the life:
Exercise each morning. Abstinence.
And sex in the afternoon, calories spent,
that one may feast by evening,
oblivious to which channel,
which batter, which inning
in what city, which trial, which riot,
which approaching storm—
yes, as if by candlelight,
this take-out in your lap,
then crème de coco for desert.

Later, should ever you not
kiss your love goodnight,
let it be not chocolate
you forgot
but appetite.

The Unclimbing

The living
dwelling
but a rung
or few
down
the ladder,
why deny
loss up top
stalks, too,
a rock dove
circling our
backyard
clearing

(flutter
and stop,
flutter
and stop,
its rush
of wings
on hinges
of rust
haunt
like an
oil-starved
wheel
on a cart)

as if trapped
in an aviary
over the spot,
that oval
of pulled
feathers
ashes
of its mate—
grackles
still
squawking,
flocking,
hastening
away,
awhile,
the hawk.

Original Self

Finally, sleep stares you in the face.

The feather of a crow falls through the dark.

Eyes closed, you glimpse the hollow of your limbs.

The Philosopher's Fireplace

What we have here's theatre.
Observe, please, that character

to the rear who, in truth, doesn't
dance so much as dies. Wasn't

that a wing it suddenly
became to magically

disappear and reappear
as another wing? What fear

might drive our affection from
the Devil's proscenium

if not the numb sensation
of having seen the whole run

in a single scene for which
the phoenix flies to then ditch

to fly again? That's its Karma.
Ours is this curtain on La-La

Land, from CNN to chain mail mesh,
before which we sit, we watch,

feel it fail to wash away
the cold hard facts of the day:

to rise is another death,
to lie is another birth;

to be unborn is the life when
to die is to drop the knife.

The Victim

When in the far flung future of this moment
an old woman sees the unspeakable events
of this morning in this, her diary, perhaps
she'll read it aloud, remembering the girl
who faithfully, all those years, held her
caught breath: today I am raped. I swear
I'll not tell a soul—even Jesus, who, could he
imagine my terror, would've spared me from it.

Yet somehow let it be known that in the midst
of the attack I became wet, that, in the event
of my passing, here is a record of my mounting
lust, which is the cold, curious urge to,
like a black widow, kill and create.

Mother, though as long as we both live
you shall not know, you are the black widow.
Father, you, her mate. May she murder you
without passion, feed your need to return
to me, which—I vow—I shall fulfill.

Increase Claflin

I, husband to my Mary, she, about whom little is known,
So that I speak from the grave of her grave countenance
In the face of all she faced, faithful to me and my wandering
Disposition, soldier I was in a line of soldiers, then overlord
Of many in my employ whom Mary kindly mothered
Along with our children as, over time, we moved from Boston
To New Orleans, then up Big Muddy to become the first
White folk to settle on the thumb of the high-held hand
That is Wisconsin, haven the Potawatomi called heaven.
In harmony we lived afore a scare. Our eldest's husband's scorn
For our neighbors' ways had him fiddling fools with firewater till
Brothers attacked, and I with my Scot's bloodline and barrel chest,
I fought back with a keg they thought was whiskey but black powder
Instead. I say unto you it is strength that staves off annihilation,
That makes for peace. As for Mary, full of charity, she knew
No privilege, save to one day send, she and I, our three sons
Off to Old Abe to help save the country and end slavery.

Words Not Mine

The words not mine: "Look. Deer,"
as one, two, three, four, five
a good ten yards apart
took flight across the road
for us to spot a sixth

emerge a quarter mile
down stream where fallen trees
obscured the melt from ice
to river, shoring up
imagination's leap

to land a memory—
green envy—Stafford's piece,
his coming upon how
a journey can not end
without it shall begin

again traveling through
the dark, his hand as if
a priest's soft touch that felt
faint heat beneath the fur,
a fawn alive but lost

inside the dead doe hit,
the unreality
of it, that pure, rapt act
that now may symbolize
no thing but what was is.

I Go to the Aviary of the Ethereal

The briefest sound of feathers,
my warm Coke flung,

wind fanning a liquid wing
in space of a camera flash

as if off thinnest carnival glass.
And here I soar standing stock-still . . . .

Conversion

for Beth Ann Fennelly

"What has sound got to do with music?"
—Charles Ives

Like a song he heard wrong all his life
thought he knew what it took to be moved,
wolves, loons plying from the spirit life,
no glimpse of it soon to be improved
upon, yet there arose from the mouth
of his being by way of being
· where he dreamed—call it North via south—
if not prayer, no craven brazen thing
less holy than in its refusal
to beseech, seek, even, the divine—
some syncopation, an interval
like a lake mirroring stars, tree line,
but outside of time, the mind at home
with the mute music of the poem.

Fly and Mirror

I sha'nt sugarcoat it.
I can't say this fly
like a circus flea
clings in a gravity defying
fling with its sweetie,

when around here
the world is far
from a ball, is
flat, domestic—hardly,
in a word, unparalleled.

Even clung to the fly,
the eye can't deny
a sourbland
face abides in place
of space, in that

the fly on the other side,
being its own fly,
also buzzes
an interior, flies off
wherever would honey

be—my doppelganger
and me shy of any—
over a shoulder,
around a corner
toward our common cupboard

made not of wood but words.

The Strip

Karl invents a comic strip in which
he becomes his own character. At first
it will not be a secret, and he sketches
it with little gusto—something to do on
a rainy Saturday for which his mate takes
no notice. Weeks pass and amazingly Karl
has a pile of drawings among work papers
he knows not how to explain. Now he
is startled when his wife walks into
the room, and he is observed quickly
shuffling his desktop should people
call to say they are stopping over.
One day some people in the comic strip
call to say they are stopping over.
Karl goes into a panic. There are
drawings flying everywhere, one of which
slips out the open window and lands
like a big leaf at Karl's wife's feet,
where she is raking. "What is this?"
she wants to know, thrusting the drawing
in the face of Karl, who's spun in
his chair next to the window where
she stands in the threshold of the door.

Terrified, Karl erases the evidence
and, since her hand holds the drawing,
also part of her arm. Soon she is standing
there, not all there, a trace of her former
self imbued with a beauty he formerly could
only imagine. Over her head Karl fashions
a light bulb dark as an eclipse of the moon.
Within a year there is a bale of paper
so thinly dispersed about their house
it cannot possibly be detected, for Karl
has long ago arrived at an answer why he
started the strip in the first place—
his desk never exactly the same in
consecutive frames, a seemingly endless
variety of kitchen aids, portraits
on the walls all originals in halls
and corridors that must wind through

space for the length it would take
decades to tour, the walls themselves
only the obverse of more walls behind
which is every model of every object he
ever desired, not the least of which is
Karl, a transformed man, drawn now
with a knowledge bump on top of his head,
the head which still houses its secret.

A Necrology

To the one that left, if not kicking,
screaming of the necessity
of forever keeping its own mouth shut,
say good night.

Good night to the slight one whose ribs shown through,
a stripper's split zipper running the length of her spine.

And to the pale sonnet
and its pale sisters,
spinsters who sang the lyrics
though learned nothing of the ways of love,
good night.

Say to the surreal,
May you reign in the interminable dream,
you for whom your lord
granted you the title "Insomnia."
And while heaven is an oligarchy
with scores more like you,
even the watchman has, deserves,
rest. Good night.

Show no mercy. Keep the concrete
bound in its misery.
"Space," especially, words both vertical
and horizontal, with lines slanting across
to form a three dimensional box,
that doodle you drew as a kid,
that glass coffin in want of a lid, a vault.

And to your blue period say good night.
For it was the time of the impossible poem.
The poem you strived without words to write
when at last you leaned into your pen,
penned   *emty*
in blue blue enough,
if not true black—Orpheus's pupil
dilating, looking
back.

Vanishing Point

A February Saturday afternoon, Heineken gone
to your head, you take the back way home,
come to a stop, flick on the blinker you forgot
that now clicks like memory's own metronome.

Swinging onto Garton Road, you catch a quarter mile ahead
a car cocked on the edge, half in the ditch, flashers,
a signal any rum-dumb son of a sailor heeds
as if heart were radar enough for head, with no hedges,

no fences along the blond/black waves of cornrows,
no trace of snow to obscure the scarred, the sacred spot
she props a new blue wreath, a slight woman or girl,
you cannot tell, as she wears a yellow hood and is thus

anonymous as the pseudo-mourners (the morbid, the curious)
these four months since the boy lost his grip on the wheel.
That he might have been dreaming, it being near midnight,
that the paper told who, what, where, yet no why

is the mystery in this miserable memorial and why
they are drawn here maybe instead of elsewhere, this
landscape where last he was alive, complete with portal,
that the pilgrim within us may spy a hidden shore and—
which?—kneel before the canvas or, at sight of it, retch.

Linda in Storage

(Denver Art Museum)

Glint of sun, a thin halo, as if rim of an abandoned
wedding band imbedded in the crown of an apple
with stem like a stamen. How odd though apropos
to think at once of *Linda*, of flowers, of a cold volcano—
that apple's dimple from whence came an
eruption, then sweet afterglow, albeit gone to regret,
source of all misery in the universe human
some would have one believe.

And that white sheet wound around Linda's middle,
serpentine, wide enough to have swallowed a child,
as though to hide her sex, to punish us with but a glimpse,
the showing a rare reprieve from her box,
for she is plastic, perhaps with a hairline crack
through which her soul escapes
if no more than molecule per minute.

Even exposed, gone is her light, now shy as noon shadow,
she who hugs the earth—calf. knee. hip. midriff twist
to chest, ear, and cheek—face toward us, underscored
by her left hand pointing to her forward flung black hair,
pupils plumbing the dark.

The Flames of the Giraffe

Hands held behind the back
won't lull the guard asleep
when so close I cloud the glass
to offer the heat my cheek,
just as diagonally, down,
the artist offers his own
to that of a delighted spouse,
espousing perhaps the virtue
of these inventions, blind to
the approval of my restraint—
monsters, guard and I, to deny
thought of a plot to possess
what, when even we have left,
still steals away the breath.

"Starving Artists Emergency Liquidation"

Because Dali meant dollars, we might suspect
he too thumbed American popular culture—
not for any Huey, Dewey, and Louie—
certainly no Long, Thomas, or Armstrong—

but Scrooge, maybe, frames that contained
something like indoor terrain
to afford us the proper perspective
so one could sense how colossal the vault;

how massive its bullion walls;
how fat the sacks of cash
stacked compact as classical columns;
and why, without a Bobcat's bucket,

there was the bulldozer, its blade
to grade coin too mountainous to count.
Yet it's retrospect that reveals
what Dali pretended not to know:

What value is currency when it won't buy time?
Hence, the liquidation of clocks,
the limp of limb, the persistence
of precision, the paranoia

that informed the pigments.
And speaking of pig mints—
none more delectable may be had of late
than on late night television, that ad touting

bargains because our artists are starving,
starring the voice calling, "Come on down"
to the Pie-in-the-Sky room,
the Airport Holiday Inn, 2 p.m., Sunday, so we

too can cash-in on emaciated artists' surplus,
properties so cold the scene's about to fold,
canvas that may not break the mold
by God but who gives a rip about old masters

when crude's to be had in our own backyard
at a discount, no less: cottages with doors
for dwarves, pale skies to match the blue flower,
still lives. But no black velvet. As if we're

not smart enough to think they think
black velvet could mean curtains for the art market.
So we wink. We sip imaginary sherry in place.
We toast the barker and his phantoms in the face:

Here's to you, starving artists, and to us:
May you be dispatched from your scrawniness.
May you eat meat, cheese, bread, and produce.
May you become so huge you fail to reproduce.

The Dream Test

for Philip Dacey

Q.

What is a dream?

a)   Elvis on an elephant on black velvet.
b)   air in there so rare you pass out.
c)   a worm-hole from which you emerge in the morning.
d)   shadows of the torch in Cranium's Cave.
e)   trying to play Scrabble in Alphabet Soup.
f)   a pack of crayons too long in the sun you color with.
g)   where penlight is spelled penis.
h)   a movie you saw you can't remember.
i)   the mind's eye's myopia.
j)   the puddle jumper's reflection.
k)   the comma in the coma we call sleep.

A.

A dream is the body gone nocturnal, the soul
folded in and upon itself, sight never seen in the flesh.

Unique Forms of Continuity in Space

Undeterred, unencumbered, unholy
mold of moiling metal, mass of golden
bronze in midst of swift stasis as it wades
ever deeper the invisible stream
recurrent as the future if space were
time, as if the engine to this stopped train
of genius locked—gone bold from bipedal.

Bold in the sense of a demon bolting
out of the ethereal and into
consciousness is bold. O in span of one
century, see at what becoming you've
indeed become, needing not hands nor arms
on your foredoomed stretch to here and beyond,
new cause for torque in your torso, for your
indignation, for your great, grave swagger.

Portrait with Toothbrush

From in the mirror there's that stare
again, that look that says how long
can this go on: what color Herr
has left is—whoa—is way just wrong.

The same applies to hazel eyes
he has, as if their bushy throng
above weren't plucked of pure-white lies
to ape the brow of yon young Kong.

As for his wooly thread-bare chest
you'd think the silver'd be on back,
except this ghostly old boy bests
his other side—in fact flat black.

So, softly off to tell the sheep,
to lift, to peek beneath the sheet
and ever so often re-bleat
with smiles to go before I sleep.

Naming the Animals

for Billy Collins

Every few months I haul Rascal to the kennel
I'm struck by the poverty of my imagination.
Here is no Spot. There's no Fido. No Pluto or Spike.

One pen might read Cobalt instead of Blue.
In another, a pair of Beagles, Calvin and Luther.
There might be a Sapo, squatting like a toad.

Then a Poodle called Dolly. A Great Dane, Ham.
You think you know when a dog's been named by an adult.
And then you come upon—no lie—Pinocchio. Hershey. Icarus.

You hear with your eye Woolf. Tundra. Big Ben.
With what ease you match the word to the breed!
The sentiment to the inner longings of the master!

Driving home, the impossible is no longer possible.
You're the one chosen to christen new species
the way the wealthy name thoroughbreds:

Mamma's Bank Account, Gerund Phase, Hopscotch.
Robert's Rule Of Anarchy, Gone Fishing, Threestrikes.
Well Like A Reservoir, Anna Maze, Habitation.

Pleas Pleas Pleas, Ticket To Ride, WCW's Wife,
The Jersey Turnpike, Sweet Hot . . . . It's days like these
you suckle one of the myriads of the muse's breasts,

knowing the Ark as the flagship in an endless line of craft.

After Hearing Lightning Strikes the Earth 100 Times per Second

I'd like to go out like this light bulb.
When I pulled the chain and it popped,
they must have seen a surge down at the power station.

Then, again, there are probably plenty of people
standing this very second with a dead light bulb in hand
maybe before a door opened to a dark attic.

Perhaps they all were as surprised as I
as I think even a blind person might experience
the sudden presence then absence of heat—

the way he'd know his picture has just been taken—
or certainly detect the music, that quick symphony,
the twinkle of a star should I ever hear a star twinkle

or—perched before the black of hell—my paltry encore,
the filament, going plink, plink, when shaken, exploded
like a dead daddy longlegs in a dusty bottle.

After Is Sometimes Before as in Now

Futures remain unchanged this morning.
      —radio

Take your own future.
Say luck has not struck.

It is the same
as yesterday morning.

While overnight
a pothole

may have surfaced
on the way to work,

all roads lead, it is said,
to Rome, coming to mean

in this millennium
carbon,

like the white dwarf
BPM 37093,

found to be all diamond,
10 billion trillion trillion

carats of diamond,
fit for the ring finger

on a child bride
of the Lord God.

On the Long-Ago Death of John Lennon

"I hate it that he is dead,"
Matthews wrote of Coleman Hawkins,
a line I've said a thousand times
since "the assassination"
so that, when I put it like that,
it makes it, Lennon's death,
sound political, as of course
it was. It doesn't require a minor
in political science to understand
politics is about power,
and powerlessness is exactly
what killed him, a .22 in the hand
of a kid so ineffectual
even his name's become a jumble.

But what I hate also is Lennon's
last words as told, I suppose,
by his widow: "I'm hit." That's
it. Hardly the line of a prince
and more like more of his clowning
around (as they all were clowns,
except the dour George, whose
serious countenance we ignored,
as he could look into the lens
and see the bullets coming,
though in retrospect we thought
at best he was tired, at worst
bored). "I'm hit." As if all
along he'd been playing Cops
and Robbers. Then Cowboys and
Indians. Then Soldier. The music,
after all, while still beautiful,
was only the envelope of the same
letter sent over and over.

"I'm hit." He must have thought
he could simply do another pirouette
and rise up singing, forgetting,
maybe, all he knew, that "Beauty
is for amateurs," (more last words
from Matthews' "A Night at the Opera")
meaning, as applied to Lennon,
our most profound work's not how
but what is said: First, you
learn it alone. And if you learn
it well, you say it from the dead.

On the Death of Harry Nilsson

That disembodied voice
trapped in a vinyl bottle
to be let loose
every so often
to like a sardonic perfume
permeate the room

I'd rather it be fog
of his ghost
in its gray sweatsuit
and hood
its back toward
than be it his face
ever since

Ghost Story

It could not be more like encountering a ghost,
this smell of damp and cold that rose off his
clothes where he stood in the middle of the room
like a pocket of fog on the dark half of a planet
that won't revolve. For he owns this night and
every night he owns a bottle. He will return as
surely as a recurring bad dream, stoke the fire,
and squat to soak up heat, interrupting the light
by which she reads her lesson, even as she did
as a young bride, feigning rapture with her Bible
in her lap, invaded by sadness and her premonition
of the loss of him, while he slowly thawed, a puddle
spreading under him as if under an old dog. Forever
she has owned the will of a willow, bowing to his
stinking desires. But now the permanent frost,
the autumn winds having stripped her bare. When he
speaks, it is as if someone is not there: "Snow's so
wet and deep I feel like I'm digging my own grave."
The willow whips the wind which whips it, she knows,
but her grief cannot bring her to hear—her Bible
no comfort, her congregation more stupidly mute than
an archangel come judgement. For she has summoned
the deacons, made them quake before her bed, mussed
by some neighbor-town strumpet. What saves her life
is the terrible knowledge that alive he is already
dead. He will go, having come back—like in an old
story—from the coast, reeking of rum and perfume.
Bent at the waist, up to his elbows in the sink, he
will wash. She will ready herself for church. There
in the mirror for the first time in forty years their
eyes will meet, and her hair dryer will fall from her
hand in a metallic whine, him unable to reveal his
surprise at the brief knowledge of the source of his
demise like lightning between his ears.

Poem in Three Movements
Beginning with a Misreading of a Line by Elizabeth Bishop

1.

Of night and flying flat on one's back, this
slow, bold, horizontal bolt of lighting
we saw course through a cloud just last evening
what else is there to say but as pure luck
would have it our sight sometimes seems trained on
the same phenomenon as if the past
might now prove truly verifiable.

2.

Of night and flying flat on one's back it
can't be said we haven't imagined new
old feats out on the lawn, lying side by
side for the sake of remembering
what it is like to swim that tired swimmer's
carry, that backstroke without the crawl,
victims of love's wave and undertow of.

3.

Of night and flying flat on one's back, first
of certain ends to which we'll come, coffin
bound, bound itself by what is called the ground,
earth, words for world or this eastward whorl
of atoms—vapor, air, water, and woods—
as known from a great distance and none, this
glimpse of night and flying flat on one's back.

Rapture

rhymes with rupture
and that's exactly what the sky does,
some would have you believe.
You know those paint chips in abandoned rooms
that lie on windowsills like bits of eggshell.
I saw the source, hole the size of a quarter,
struck as I was by the older, darker blue beneath,
that corollary of another soul
escaped to her maker
where surely it was warmer
this Christmas day,
heat here only high enough
to preserve the pipes
the years she'd wintered elsewhere,
driven herself there, the county home,
to check herself in.

You see, we were in my brother-in-law's
ninety-two-year-old-grandmother's house, eerily
empty despite his family, my brother's, mine
and my mother, rummaging around, the furniture
intact, junk neatly stacked
on the dining room table for the taking,
down to her address book, blank in spots
though not where my thumb stopped
the pages that sputtered under it:
"police."

Slowly we dispersed but first just stood,
thinking, maybe, like me, how a house
without bread is not a home
(I'd come upon my mother before a bare cupboard).

Then, with my nephew of four, I took the tour.

"Right here is where she died," he said
at a worn spot on the carpet.
His cousins, of course, had lied.
But I made my eyes go wide, saw
on a wall a picture of her church,
and caught on the floor still another pile,
her Bible on top.

Here were the real remains, I thought
and thought how odd the body is decked
with her best jewelry
instead of the good book.

I suppose we left as hopeful as not.

After the holidays, halted at a toll booth
half way home,
I read a red bumper sticker ahead:

IN CASE OF RAPTURE
THIS VEHICLE WILL BE UNMANNED.

I thought of the nerve,
the fear.
I thought then of the house,
the line on everyone's mind:
"The place has possibilities."

We drove off.

And looking back, I saw the earth.

A Short History of History

There was that which we couldn't possibly
understand, though we did—new words for war
and none for peace. The text didn't exist
whose author could speak the minds of angels,
their lexicon of love smothered by weight
of the archaic, with so many ghosts
and, relatively, so little paper
in the world. About two thousand years' worth
of paper. That's all. That's it. If only
more of those pages could hold any hope,
a buried "Help!-Being-held-hostage" note
or an honest "Wish-you-were-here" to an
anonymous future, we might say of
history it's less like butcher paper
than bond, even a whole new rolled scroll—blank,
on a hollow spool, and not black with blood.

In a Rain I Hit Root

Sometimes I forget why I'm here,
it being, for one, to mop contents
of a newly bought bottle of Woolite—

its top not on tight—promptly dropped.
But all's right, far from life's last
mishap, groundwater no worse off

when, through a bit of ingenuity
and engineering on a shirt box,
I scraped, scooped, sent soap

on a slow though slick descent
to the wastewater treatment plant that,
as if studying a turned back clock,

I've thought about a lot of late,
thought on the walk I take
of a route I used to jog with the dog.

The dog's gone, wrapped in a green
fitted sheet three feet down
where near dawn in a rain I hit root.

Sometimes I remember why I'm here
when I'm there, mud up to my ankles,
just off the path back of the house,

seeing Wade, brow hidden by his bowed head,
shuffling toward, cradling that green bundle.
Surely it's not shame turning me again

from this recurring rain of grief,
but that morning we did not hug,
we did not touch, as though to do so

might undermine an unspoken belief
whatever a son is tall enough to carry
a father ought not but shallow bury.

Negative Capability

for Marion Stocking

Wife off to work, I awaken late, punch on CNN,
make the bed, hear in the background
of the movement for the canonization of Padre Pio.

It's not the bleeding, not the power of healing.
It's he's said to have had the capacity
of being in more than one place at once,

out distancing, I think, the Road Runner maybe,
who, had I satellite on a Sunday morning,
might be up there on a couple of channels,

and I think of both my sons, now grown, out on their own,
yet on my mind. Downstairs on the kitchen counter,
I'm able to predict, any list of what needs to be fixed

is nixed. Neither is it like Bill's note to Flossie with plums
gone from the icebox. "Happy Father's Day," the note
will say. "Decide where you want to go out to eat."

Mile and a half into the morning's walk
I stop at a painted turtle trying to climb the curb,
three legs swimming the air, only to pivot

and fall back. Years ago I would have carried him home
to my kids. Why now do I not stoop to rescue,
as if I believed the revolving Earth and chance

a better caretaker? On a bookshelf in the Vatican
there are six bound volumes in support of the beatification
of Padre Pio. If my inertia were but one page of that

we might say of the father he was a quack,
not that anyone says *this* father was a quack.
I've twice tried mass, in fact. Which is pretty good

for a Protestant, I'd bet, a former Protestant, that is—
"Methodist" stamped in tin and strung on my key chain,
the one thing I kept the Army gave me—complete

with name, serial number, blood type—as though
if I ever got shot, out on my walk, they'd know who,
what not to hang, and not to call a priest,

that I probably don't want a vet or the president but
the god of A positive. Not that I've never believed.
This I did and do believe: I believe in the power

of fathers to screw up their sons. Consider
the case of the author of the ad I'll call
The Billboard with the Black Background on Calumet:

> Have you read my #1
> best seller? There will be
> a test.   —God

With a season in hell inferred, how's that
for two syllables shy of a haiku? Recalling it,
sans title, from a year ago, now I know where

I don't want to go: anywhere they serve turtle soup.
For heaven would be hell without home.
As to the test, I figure it would be true/false—

no multiple choice—as well as pass/fail.
And while I'd not earn a hundred,
I'm not anti-sainthood, though most of the time,

unlike Padre Pio and with sons as my witness,
I hesitated. I hovered over what is best.
I dwelled in more than one place at once.

Sommer's Fur Farm

Were I to follow this homemade
logo on its truckbed of plywood
empty almost as the crates it carries
ignoring even my turn-off for work
surely would be revealed a lane
mud ruts with sunflowers
on one side and corn on the other
winding like a dry creekbed
to conifers surrounding outbuildings
and a barn in the dead of Wisconsin.

I might speak now of a black caterpillar
crawling on the skull of a bald man
cows that cough up hair balls
a mink pitch fork
the bearskin rug
in the farmer's den and
the fur-lined cups and saucers
in the kitchen we sip
pretend cups of coffee from
picking in midst of conversation
first fuzz and now dust from the bread.

Merging

off an overlong
on-ramp, foot
nearly to floorboard,
radio on—The Doors'
 "L.A. Woman,"
Morrison's voice
gone raucous
with velocity
as if score
for the mini indie
in your mirror:
blurred billboard
diminishing, trees
shrinking, median
tapering, backs
of traffic signs
swallowed—
clouds, even sky
drawn into the past,
spawning recollection
of a narrowing
riverscape,
its exponentially
swift drift toward
the falls, while
you and your luck
hurl into the future,
pavement
conveyor belt
hauled out
from under you.

Air Lock

A space odyssey this is not, though in midst
of another blasted trip, wife and I,
for the U.W. Clinic, made to reminisce
over last month's glimpse of how ultrasound
can turn a pocket of the universe inside out
already up side down: a college son's rare syndrome,
"Thoracic Outlet," with "a clot the size of a brat,"
that flock of doctors' hospital talk,
his only symptom sudden, "classic,"
(brought on in an Eddie Bauer trying a sweater on),
his left arm gone purple as grape popsicle.
And though it seemed we missed this Christmas,
cold as hell, we needed no fleece and,
thankfully, received none.

◊

Now, as if detainees we've made of ourselves,
early for the appointment, we linger
until lingering turns to dwell
in an air lock on the far edge of Fond du Lac where—
with or without needing to eat—
we ate, hands still bearing the trace
of Bacon Burgers and Curly Fries.
Forgive me, should you think there ought
not to be surprise. I take a quick glance
at my wife's eyes, big, beautiful, blue,
that just happen to have been
for thirty-three years eyes of a C.C.R.N.,
eyes that will hear no lies—
my eyes.

◊

Zipping up, slowly slipping on gloves,
it's as if we're looking around for the rocks
in this superheated box a southern-most sun
at its zenith turns to sauna, when in truth
we loiter for warmth that cannot be had between us
until this thing is done, our son is cured,
the operation a success, no need for a second one.
Finally, we run for the car, cross a white wind,
a gust's rush of nothingness
enveloping us like a ghost-herd of horses.
I step on more horses, her 300M, for heat.
Halfway across state, though we cannot know it,
awaits a slate clean of complications.
We've been to see the Wizard. One of us maybe prayed.
We're off for the specialist's, pilot
to co-pilot, mum.

◊

On the way home, somewhere around repairs
on Highway 151, just as, one right after another,
reflectors flare, steering us clear
of on-coming cars, I find my tongue,
but see by dashlight she's asleep. So
I tell myself what I might have told her,
why I have not wept or, even in relief,
weep. Outside it's zero on the overhead console,
though we're here warm, cruise control on,
hurling through space as if in place.
Like the interior, it occurs to me,
Earth's an air lock where zero's absolute.
In an hour, maybe, we'll pull into the garage,
park, another air lock. Out of one into another,
whether we make it there or not.
Now tell me, dear wife, what one of us is without
a sorrowful sense of life?

Exterior with Raised Garage Door as Proscenium

Street light for backlight stage right.

As for suspense,
unlike its audience,
the night knows not what a wish is.

It rained pinstripes.
It rained needles then nails.

It rained slapping tappets
and wax paper you'd tear
to wad in awe of a turbulent god
over and over,
a scare enough to saturate
the martyr's most dapper diaper.

When after an hour it wore away chalk
to a great glob of gray,
that glacier bone gone ghost,
our lawn's big rock,
only then we thought
how it stopped the clock,
the interval between far-away flash
and flunder—any wonder asunder.

Now the rain is water heard
as a herd of mologluels,
its fuel visible yet invisible, distinct,
like wildebeest instinct,
never here nor there,
commuting its commute
via concrete, via gutter to grate
to under ground and beyond
where it shall live for a time with the fishes
and ever, like the night, know not what a wish is.

You, Absent Your Work

Early morning
and you're a man looking over your shoulder
at whether anyone's there
to hear you talking to yourself,
not a soul here,
not even your shadow,
immersed in the shade of the building
cast beyond the vacant parking lot
like a watermark on the trees.

It has not been a particularly bad night,
yet you have arrived
before anyone else,
door agape on your car
parked several steps
from where you linger,
hands empty of briefcase,
lunch bag, thermos.

Now the air overhead is warm and liquid
yet subtle as the morning dove's call
were you a reed tugged by a spring
feeding a deep quarry
so that, if not waves,
ripples swell
as though a boy dipping his toe in Lake Michigan
might be sensed years later
by himself as an old man
waist high in the Mediterranean.

Ode in the Key of O

Kudos unto the code and to the mind
behind the hand that moved not out of need
but what must be acknowledged as a thought
nonpareil—stone turned wheel no exception—
the crude scrawl in ashes, sand, and soil
with stick or staff that which it did not know
to call symbol, yet would bring to recall
the awe uttered as o on the rounded
mouth below the eyes of one fixed upon
the moon's shape, if not in worship, wonder.

Yea, as if a remnant of gods gone ghost
gleaned from the air by the hand of a mime,
like approximation of perfection,
that diminutive orb wholly without
substance rolled from the tongue, made corporal
by yet another eidolon, the line—
call it divine insight when the pupil
of the mind's eye eclipses iris to
highlight, through swift abstraction, the concrete.

Ought it then not be, after the grand span
of five hundred generations, given
the cuneiform-like illusion of form
born of the fact of annularity,
all alacrity to the degree it
has not atrophied to hilarity
at the writ of the clock is—while more
minute each minute—worthy, too, of praise?

For value in its purest form is less
a matter of matter than the marriage
of light and shade, their interdependency
in the sense, say, male and female were one
from the beginning—no little arrow
on the o of that embryo, no foe,
target, cross, or stickman Atlas below.

Lo, behold: lift like Sol's soul o from god
there's no g. d. (or even dad gummed) thing
to which we cling if not—a la lingua
franca more so than the thing itself, life
buoy or lasso—awe, the ineffable
grasped as we're pulled, gasping, through h. to o.

Thus, as it's said, at the apogee of one's
gestation there is the crowning; there is
as well the splash, and there is the circle
of attendants, the cry, the swaddling,
the mother's embrace, infant to her breast.

Yet, birth is life's twist: in time time doesn't
exist, now flanked by nothing of the past,
no word of the future when, alas, love's
orismo's most fierce in fear of life's loss.

O, of the holes in the whole of our knowledge
we say miracle, though the miracle,
mother of miracles, is we say it.

As for love's spell—phallic l, mellow o
vis-à-vis Eve's cleft v v. snake eye e—

is it not awe to which we owe our awe?

Arboreal

Life only as full as it is empty,
you've chosen this lot, as if now sitting
cross-legged, fixed on a huge hickory,
without thought, the tree caught growing a ring.

Thing is . . . beneath trees you can't always see
above, the soundest mind opines, nor wring
the self of the ken of identity
when light's lost, insight sought in the squinting.

Which degree on your watch's three-sixty
shall no such thing as time's revved chainsaw sing
TIM-BER!, stir you aware this is the *thee*
blur—the snap, crackle, and whump—come crashing?

Whether hear it here or on heaven's ground
depends upon definition of sound.

Notes on Phobias

Acro: heights

Agora: open spaces

Anemo: wind

Batho: depths

Cardio: heart attack

Chero: joy

Claustro: confinement

Corpro: excrement

Emeto: vomit

Grapho: writing

Hiero: religious objects

Ombro: storms

Ornitho: birds

Poly: many things

Rhabdo: punishment

Scio: shadows

Acknowledgements

Magazines

Ark River Review, Ascent, Autumn Journal, Bat City Review, Beloit Poetry Journal, Bowwow, Birmingham Poetry Review, Black Warrior Review, Borderlands, Bramble, California State Poetry Quarterly, Charter Oak Review, Chawed Rawzin, Chicago Review, Colorado-North Review, Comstock Review, Cottonwood Review, Crab Creek Review, Dacotah Territory, Eclipse, Folio, Free Verse, Freshwater, G. W. Review, Greenfield Review, Grimoire, Grand Valley Review, High Plains Literary Review, Indiana Review, Kansas Quarterly, Kavitha, Lake Superior Review, Lakeland, Lakes & Prairies, Laurel Review, Mangrove, Marquee, Mikrokosmos, Mississippi Valley Review, The Mirror, National Poetry Review, Passages North, Phantasmagoria, Poem, Poet and Critic, Poetry And, Poetry for the Masses, Poetry Hall, Poetry Now, Poets On:, qarrtsiluni, Rhode Island Review, River City, Road Apple Review, Rosebud, Runes, The Sandhills & Other Geographies, Scree, Seems, Sparrow, Spectaculum, Spoon River Quarterly, Stoneboat, Sycamore Review, Transactions, Three Rivers Poetry Journal, Translation Review, Wake: Great Lakes Thought and Culture, Washington Square, West Coast Poetry Review, Winewood Journal, Wisconsin Poets' Calendar, Wisconsin Review, and Verse Wisconsin.

Anthologies

Half Way to the North Pole. Four Windows Press. Sturgeon Bay. 2020.

Trees in a Garden of Ashes. Local Gems Press. Long Island. 2020.

Universal Oneness: An Anthology of Magnum Opus Poems from Around the World. Authorspress. New Delhi. 2020.

Poets to Come. Local Gems Press. Long Island. 2019.

Verse Daily. [www.versedaily.org]. Sunnyvale. 2019.

Bards Against Hunger. Local Gems Press. Long Island. 2018.

Ice Cream Poems. World Enough Writers. Tillamook. 2017.

This Barbed Heart: A BPJ Chad Walsh Prize Anthology. Farmington. 2016.

Intersections: Art & Poetry. Sheboygan Visual Artists and Mead Public Library Poetry Circle. Sheboygan. 2016.

How Higher Education Feels: Commentaries on Poems That Illuminate Emotions in Learning and Teaching. Brill. Leiden. 2016.

Making It Speak: Poets and Artists in Cahoots! EBCO Artworks. Sheboygan. 2014.

Cthulhu Haiku and Other Mythos Madness. Popcorn Press. Elkhorn. 2013.

Echolocations. Cowfeather Press. Madison. 2013.

Halloween Haiku. Popcorn Press. Elkhorn. 2011.

Journaling the Apocalypse. Phonenicia Publishing. Montreal. 2009.

Cadence of Hooves: A Celebration of Horses. Yarroway Mountain Press. Igo. 2008.

Poetry Daily Essentials. Sourcebooks. Naperville. 2007.

Encore. Parallel Press. Madison. 2006.

Sacred Fire. Adams Media. Avon. 2005.

The Best American Poetry 2005. Scribner. New York. 2005.

Verse Daily. [www.versedaily.org]. Sunnyvale. 2005.

Poetry Daily. [www.poems.com] Charlottesville. 2005.

Sacred Waters. Adams Media. Avon. 2005.

Dirt. The New Yinzer. Pittsburg. 2004.

Poetry Daily. [www.poems.com] Charlottesville. 2004.

And We the Creatures. Dream Horse Press. San Jose. 2003.

Poetry Daily. [www.poems.com] Charlottesville. 2003.

September 11, 2001: American Writers Respond. Etruscan Press. Wilkes-Barre. 2002.

A Fine Excess: Fifty Years of the Beloit Poetry Journal. BPJ. Farmington. 2000.

The Pushcart Prize XXV: Best of the Small Presses. W. W. Norton & Co. New York. 2000.

The Best American Poetry 2000. Scribner. New York. 2000.

Wisconsin Poetry. Wisconsin Academy of Sciences, Arts, and Letters. Eau Claire. 1991.

Poets On: Tenth Anniversary. Poets On:. Mill Valley. 1986.

The Best of the Spoon River Quarterly. Spoon River Press. Peoria. 1980.

Poems: Prairie Style. DeKalb Arts Committee. 1980.

"The Baffle" was printed as a broadside upon occasion of the author's
  induction to Lakeland University's Fine Arts Gallery of Distinction.
  January 27, 2017. Design by Monique Brickham.

In Particular

As for persons, while a list here would be distastefully long, it would begin,
of course, with Brenda.